A Daughter's Promise
By Fran Lewis

"Heartfelt and emotionally wrenching, A Daughter's Promise *is a story of life and love set against a metaphorical journey that rings with optimism against a backdrop of the impossible toll a disease like Alzheimer's has on a family. Fran Lewis's beautifully written tale spares not a single word in finding light amid a growing and pervasive darkness, even as it salvages hope from despair. This is* Tuesdays with Morrie *for a new generation, a brilliant depiction in fact of what Nicholas Sparks does so well in fiction."*
—Jon Land, *USA Today* bestselling author

"This memoir of Alzheimer's is unflinching in its honesty. At times, it is so raw that you may want to look away — but don't, because the pain of this story is outweighed by its courage, devotion, and love."
—Brian Freeman, Amazon bestselling author

Fran Lewis

"This is an amazing book because it deals with the onset and development of Alzheimer's from the standpoint of both the patient and the family member who is a caregiver. The writing is sensitive and insightful as the point of view shifts between these two. It superbly explains the many ramifications of the emotionally wrenching issue of whether to move a loved one to a nursing facility or to keep them at home. I would heartily recommend this as essential reading for so many people dealing with these very difficult and heart breaking issues."
—**Allan Topol,** national bestselling author

"In her new book, A Daughter's Promise, Fran shares a personal and emotional journey she shared with her mother. Fran shares with the readers the moment they realized that Fran's mother was suffering from Alzheimer's, to their last moments together. Fran tells the story from both of their perspectives, giving the reader unique insight to the challenges for those who suffer from this disease and for the loved ones who support them. This is more than a mother-daughter story; it is a story filled with wonderful life lessons."
—**Michael Tabman**, retired FBI agent and author of *Bad Intent, Walking the Corporate Beat, and Midnight Sin*

"A heart-wrenching first-person true story about the ravages of Alzheimer's. Told in a biography/autobiography style, the reader gets a first-hand account from the one afflicted and the one charged to be caregiver. Fran Lewis has a talent for framing and discussing Alzheimer's in a way that will resonate with people of all ages. This disease will affect all of us in one way or another. Fran paints a beautiful picture of the harsh realities and of the courage and fortitude required to face them."
—**Mark Shaff,** author of *Redemption Road* and *Force Ten*

A Daughter's Promise

"Insightful, impactful, and inspirational! Thank you for this invaluable resource for all ages. Kudos to you for being a real promise keeper! Ruthie groomed you to record and broadcast this incredible journey behind the veil of a mind tormented by intruders. Thanks for the helpful lessons provided for caregivers, seniors, family members and health care providers."

—**Gloria Shell Mitchell,** author of *The Garbage Man's Daughter* series, *My Knotty Decision, Bliss and Blisters in Love & Marriage,* and *Desire After Divorce*

"A touching tale of a woman's struggle with Alzheimer's, from the onset of the disease to the loss of her sense of self. Told from both her and her daughter's perspectives, Ruth's own words lay bare the incompetence of care providers, the creeping realization of what's happening to her, and finally the recognition of where it's leading. A Daughter's Promise *gives important insight into a disease that robs the victim of the core of what makes us who we are as individuals. If you've ever wondered what it's like from the afflicted's point of view, this book is a must-read."*

—**Alan Jacobson,** *USA Today* bestselling author of the FBI profiler Karen Vail series

Published by EditPros LLC
423 F Street, Suite 206
Davis, CA 95616
www.editpros.com

ISBN: 978-1-937317-40-9 (print)
ISBN: 978-1-937317-41-6 (ebook)
Library of Congress Control Number: 2017950434

Printed in the United States of America

ABOUT THE COVER:

Ruth Swerdloff's 1945 graduation photo from
Roosevelt High School in the Bronx.

Table of Contents

Dedication

To the memory of Ruth Swerdloff, whose journey you are about to take.

Many people fall into routines that require them to do the same thing, the same way, everyday. They get up, go to work and perform the same job, read the same types of books—never changing anything. When they are forced to vary from their routines, some people often find it difficult, or virtually impossible. People, not just seniors, who take part in different activities each day give their minds a chance to workout, which may reduce their risk of developing dementia. This book is dedicated to all those whose memories are precious, whose lives have been drastically changed, and whose families I hope after reading this book will understand the huge undertaking and commitment they are making when they decide to become a caregiver. In my heart and soul, I hope someday a cure or a preventive will be found for Alzheimer's disease. I dedicate this book to my mom, Ruth Swerdloff, who gave me the courage to be the person I am today, and taught me the true meanings of courage and survival.

Special dedication to Stacy Modlin for reading my book, giving me positive feedback, and re-editing it. You are the best, and I will always hold you dear as one of my favorite and closest cousins in the world. -Frani

Preface

According to the Mayo Clinic, Alzheimer's disease is a degenerative brain disorder that impacts memory, thinking skills and other important cognitive functions.

Dementia isn't a specific disease. Rather, dementia describes a group of symptoms affecting memory, thinking and social abilities severely enough to interfere with daily functioning.

Dementia indicates problems with at least two brain functions, such as memory loss, impaired judgment or language, and the inability to perform some daily activities, such as paying bills or driving.

Alzheimer's disease is the most common cause of dementia. In Alzheimer's disease, brain cells degenerate and die, causing a steady decline in memory serious enough to interfere with everyday life. Alzheimer's medications can help, for a time, with memory symptoms and other cognitive changes, but they don't prevent Alzheimer's disease from progressing.

An important first step in developing a treatment plan for any disease is having a clear diagnosis. New Alzheimer's tests may help with early detection of some of the pathological components of the disease. However, before these become widely available, more research is needed to determine who might benefit from them and what they reveal about the progression of Alzheimer's and other diseases.

- Biomarker test. Researchers have proposed Alzheimer's tests that measure two proteins, beta-amyloid and tau, in cerebrospinal fluid. The fluid is examined for evidence of abnormal development of beta-amyloid proteins, which form plaques, and tau proteins, which form tangles. Both plaques and tangles are thought to contribute to the development of Alzheimer's disease. These proteins can help identify people with the underlying disease process who are likely to progress to more–serious forms of the disease.

- Brain imaging (neuroimaging). Brain imaging—using equipment to record images of changes in the brain—is another area of research. Researchers are studying imaging techniques, such as magnetic resonance imaging (MRI) and positron emission tomography (PET) scans, used in conjunction with radiotracers. These radiotracers are charged particles that "light up" Alzheimer's-affected areas in images of the brain—for example, by attaching to proteins, amyloid and tau, associated with Alzheimer's disease.

- Cognitive assessment. Technology is also being used to develop software for computer–based assessments that detect cognitive changes and may be useful in the early diagnosis of Alzheimer's disease.

Early detection and diagnosis of Alzheimer's disease is an important goal. Early intervention with medications may slow the progression of the disease and provide a better opportunity to plan for the future.

The Alzheimer's Foundation of America (https://alzfdn.org) offers the following information on its website for the detection of Alzheimer's disease, and the common stages of the disease:

What are signs and symptoms of Alzheimer's disease?

Although each individual is unique, experts have identified common warning signs of Alzheimer's disease, including:

- Memory loss, especially of recent events, names, places and other new information
- Confusion about time and place
- Struggling to complete familiar tasks such as brushing one's teeth
- Trouble finding appropriate words, for example in a sentence

- Difficulties in judging situations
- Changes in mood and personality

What are the stages of Alzheimer's disease?

Alzheimer's Foundation of America follows the National Institutes of Health's National Institute on Aging in describing the disease in three stages early (mild), middle (moderate) and late (severe).

Early (Mild)

In this stage, people may:

- Forget words or misplace objects
- Forget something they just read
- Ask the same question over and over
- Have increasing trouble making plans or organizing
- Not remember names when meeting new people

Middle (Moderate)

In this stage, people may have:

- Increased memory loss and confusion
- Problems recognizing family and friends
- Continuously repeating stories, favorite wants (e.g., foods, places, songs, etc.), or motions

- Decreased ability to perform complex tasks (e.g., planning dinner) or handle personal finances (e.g., paying bills)
- Lack of concern for hygiene and appearance
- Requiring assistance in choosing proper clothing to wear for day, season, or occasion

Late (Severe)

In this stage, there is almost total memory loss. The individual may:

- Recognize faces but forget names
- Mistake a person for someone else
- Delusions—such as thinking he/she needs to go to work — may set in, even though he/she no longer has a job
- There is a strong need for holding something close for tactile stimulation, nurturing, companionship and comfort
- Basic abilities such as eating, walking, and sitting up fade during this period; the individual may no longer recognize when he is thirsty or hungry and will need help with all basic activities of daily living.

Fran Lewis

Part One

A Daughter's Promise

Fran Lewis

Reading has always been the way for me to escape to other worlds, learn about many different places, and expand my knowledge of so many subjects. With a notepad in hand and several pens at the ready, I begin reading the many books that authors send me each day. Detailing the plot, the characters, and taking notes throughout, I create a perfect analysis of the book.

Remembering what my mom had told me, to always look for that special message in the book and create that first paragraph to stimulate reader interest, I begin my review. Perfection: that's what she always told me. Each piece of writing, each assignment had to be done to the standards set by my teachers and professors, and then pass the highest test, mom's. I remember coming out of school one night, and she stuck her hand out waiting to see what I'd gotten on my midterm in one of my graduate courses in administration. I still smile when I remember what happened. I left out one question and got a 98, and I told mom what I did wrong and the right answer. But, the professor was so frustrated with most of the other students that she had to revamp the scores by adding ten points to everyone's test scores just to have more students pass, so mom was satisfied with my 108. And, of course, on the final I did get 100 and an A in the class, because it was what was expected of me by myself, and of course, mom.

Till this day I still create my reviews, my schedule for my radio show, and anything else that I decide to venture into, like the *MJ* magazine in memory of my sister Marcia Joyce, with the understanding that my work has to stand up to the highest standards. The articles, reviews, stories, and issues that are published should be equal to those of any credible magazine on the newsstands.

So, mom, it's been five years and it seems like yesterday. I hope I will continue to make you proud of me. You taught me well. Yes, I never leave the house without looking my best. You were my mom, my mentor, and my best friend. You will always be here for me in spirit.

Today you would have celebrated your 89th birthday with a special red rose and your favorite chocolate cake. Your blue eyes and your great smile would light up the room, and of course the presents we would give you would make you proud. You taught us never to give up on our dreams, nor settle for less than we want in our lives. You made sure that you listened when we felt down and needed a guiding hand to rise back up. You never faltered and never passed judgment. You were our mother, our guide, and our best friend. Rules were made and enforced, but never with an iron hand. Explanations were given for your requests, and we all followed suit and showed you the respect you deserved.

When you became ill we all rallied together as a family to make sure you remained at home and received great help. We were truly blessed to have Joyce, Joan, Laurel, Pat, Tessa, Loretta, and Getty to take such good care of you and, of course, someone we all miss and loved, Veronica Collins, your case manager, who made sure that you were safe and protected by the best aides in the world from Partners in Care. So, mom, happy birthday, and let the sun shine tomorrow so we know that you are still watching over us and protecting

Marcia, who is with you now. We miss your wisdom, your guidance, the huge grey mobile that you drove anywhere you were needed, as the taxi driver for your friends, and the orange mobile that my reading students loved when you picked me up or drove me to school. I made a promise and vowed that I would do everything in my power to care for you, keep your mind and body active, and never even consider the one thing so many others do, placing you in a nursing home.

The circle of life begins on the day you are born and ends when you close your eyes for the last time and take your last precious breath.

Ruth Swerdloff started her life on November 22, 1927, and became a part of a loving, nurturing family that would remain intact for the first two years of her life until the loss of her mother, when things would change. But, Ruth was special from the start, and although facing her first obstacle at the age of two, losing a parent, she somehow learned to accept the change with the help of her sister, Tova, and three brothers, Kenny, Irving, and Harry. This is her story. This is where her circle of life begins.

Part Two

A Startling Revelation

Fran

Sitting in the diner having breakfast with my mom changed the course of my life forever. Hearing her tell me that she felt something within her mind and body was changing, and that she could no longer remember certain dates, facts, or even places where she had recently been, frightened her. It also alerted her to the fact that something was happening and she needed to investigate what it was, but had no idea how.

Throughout my life she taught me values and stood firm on what she expected of me, my sister, and my brother, at all times. Veering from what she had mapped out for each one of us was out of the question. But on this day she wanted to understand why adding simple numbers was no longer possible. Why she could not remember names and places, and all too often she was starting to drive on the wrong side of the road, or pass through red lights, saying she was in a hurry and did not have time to stop for the other cars.

Hearing her say this, I began thinking of what I'd learned or knew about dementia/Alzheimer's, and decided I would research how people with memory problems could regain some of what they had lost, and how I could help her remember some of the people, places, and dates. So, I took out a notepad and asked her to do me a favor and add up some bills that I had with me, hoping that her bookkeeping skills would kick in.

I had some simple cleaning tickets, and asked her to add two at a time to help me find out how much I owed the several cleaners that I frequented. The results were not good. Choices had to be made. Her life was about to change, and the decision, although uniform and agreed upon by my sister and brother, was mine. The choices were discussed as to whether to enlist the help of aides from an agency, or place her in a facility. Both my sister and brother struggled with the decision, but ultimately the decision was mine to care for her at home, knowing that the burden of care would be mine.

Part Three

Where My Life Declined: When Alzheimer's Took Over

Ruth

My world changed when Alzheimer's came my way.

The visions I saw were no longer the way they were before.

I could not remember the simplest things, or realize or know why birds have wings.

The light in my eyes grew dimmer, as your memory had just a touch of glimmer.

My world became my inner thoughts and expressing how I felt or wanted, or my needs.

As I write, dictate these words, I realize that someone now has to help me with the simplest deeds.

7

My thoughts changed and others now have to help me make it through.

Without them I do not know what I would do!

My world changed because Alzheimer's made its rounds.

It decided to land within me in leaps and bounds.

I tried and never gave up on myself and fighting every step of the way.

Remembering that life would be different from then on, each and every day.

My world changed each minute of every day. I looked around and hoped someone would show me the way.

To remembering the good times and the people that mattered to me each day.

My world involved decisions that others had to make for me.

But, the love of those who made them always came shining through, you see.

The one thing that never changed was my spirit to survive.

No matter what the doctors predicted I remained alert and alive.

My world might have changed and was quite a blow to me, how true,

But, one thing for sure, the best of me came straight from all of you.

*Marcia might be in Heaven, but when the sun comes out
I know she is there,*

*Watching over all of us, with you together the job she does
share.*

*My world changed, but most remember I was PTA
president, bookkeeper, chauffeur, and more.*

*My friends loved me and remember me; their glowing
words I keep deep inside of me and will forever store.*

*My smile, they still say, brightened an entire room. I
never complained, ever.*

*I managed to keep my sense of humor, which to many
was a difficult endeavor.*

*My life was complete and fulfilled, because I had three
children and a husband who was the best,*

*A mom that is loved with more than words can express,
and I know that you are finally at peace and at rest.*

As Doc would always say to me in each and every rhyme,

*I might not be the same person right now, but I will love
each one of you till the very end of time.*

Part Four
Who Was Ruth?

Fran

Ruth Swerdloff, whose spirit lives on and whose family loved her tons, from the moon to the shining stars, and back.

My mom's life was not about money, vacations, or expensive cars. She did not need diamonds, furs, or high-end furniture or to live in a mansion, although she deserved all those things, and much more. She always said that she was the richest mother and woman on this earth, because she had the most wonderful and devoted family. All she ever wanted was her family to come and visit her, call her, and eat her famous brisket and chicken on the holidays.

Devoted to my dad, who everyone called "Doc," her

children, her parents, and every family member, she never forgot—and made sure we didn't forget—every birthday, anniversary, or special occasion that warranted a gift or a card. If someone needed help, no matter the cost, time, or sacrifice to herself, she was always there. Everyone was equal, and everyone counted.

Before my mom was diagnosed with Alzheimer's disease, she was active in many organizations. She was involved in National Jewish Women as their secretary. I loved attending meetings with her and my Aunt Tova. The respect she received was amazing. Another organization that she worked for, by the way, for no monetary gain, was Women's American ORT (Organization for Rehabilitation through Training). The American arm of ORT, founded in 1922, was originally only open to men. Dolowitz and Boudin, who were married to ORT officers, founded WAO to assist in funding ORT programs that were intended to help Eastern European Jews devastated by World War I. Starting with fundraising concerts and bazaars, WAO grew in response to the rise of Nazism and the plight of Jewish refugees.

Women's American ORT became an independent organization in 1940, helping to fund International ORT's growing number of vocational high schools in

Europe, India, Israel, and North Africa. Today WAO focuses primarily on fundraising for ORT schools and programs around the world, including schools in New York, Los Angeles, and Chicago. These programs help disadvantaged individuals and communities become self-sufficient by providing education and training in employment skills.

My mom loved working for this organization whose goals are clearly to foster women's rights, give scholarships to students in need of help, and working to eliminate something so prevalent in this world, anti-Semitism.

Dear Mom: You were more precious than the rarest diamond. You were my voice growing up, and I was proud to be yours while you were ill. This is for you:

Mother's have special qualities making each one unique;

Listener, adviser, consultant so to speak.

When things get tough and problems arise for you,

The solutions are always found in the wisdom of a mom, how very true.

Problem solver, taxi driver, chauffeur, bookkeeper, and coordinator was our mom, Ruth,

The force behind our success, if you want to know the honest truth.

Planning each day, outlining and scheduling every minute you see,

Mapping out a blueprint for success for my sister, brother, and me.

Organizer, leader, facilitator, PTA president, and much more,

Commanding respect from all that knew her when she walked through the door.

Mother, arbitrator, best friend, grandmother, confidant, lawyer, and accountant for all,

Whether the job was small or large, you just had to give our Ruthie a call.

Activity planner, sister, great-grandmother, you see,

Wearing different hats to help everyone, especially my sister, brother, and me.

Career guidance counselor, business director, and decision maker for my dad and the three of us,

When Ruth decided what you should do with your life, you listened and followed without any fuss.

A PhD in being a mom, she did surely earn,

All the courses in college could not teach anyone what she had already learned.

From piano lessons to violin, dancing, ice-skating, bowling lessons she gave to us all,

Recitals, Hebrew, and let's not forget my debut in

Rockefeller Center, where I had my famous fall.

Always there to dry our tears, allay our fears, and listen to our complaints and woes,

Ruth Swerdloff was a mom who far surpassed anyone that I will ever know.

Every move we made was choreographed, directed, and created by our mom to make us the best we could be.

Landing my Dad at nineteen years old was her greatest coup, you see.

For all that you did for us, I am proud to say on this sad day,

Mom: You made us strong, kind, and understanding like you in every way.

Life's journey has ended, and a new one begins wherever you are,

Know that we will all meet again and that you are never that far.

So Mom, as Dad would say every time he wrote you a special rhyme,

Dear Ruthie, Mom, Riffy, Rifkam, we will all love you till the very end of time.

Part Five
The Bitter Truth

Fran

That day in the diner rings so true within my thoughts even today. My mom cried bitter tears, realizing that this moment might be gone and more would be coming where she would forget and not be able to function. How would I make this promise to never put her in a nursing home? This is one promise I made on my own, and to everyone reading my words and hearing her voice, I hope that this book and what I have written will help anyone that has a parent, grandparent, child, aunt, or uncle hit by this dreadful disease to understand it from the viewpoint of the caregivers and the person that will never be the same.

Chapter One

How It All Began
From the Start

I created this book from the years of personal journals that my mother kept from the moment she realized something was wrong. She wanted everyone to get to know her as a person, so she started with a brief autobiography of her life. But first, here are the words that she recorded in 2002. She realized that something was dreadfully wrong, and each day she began forgetting not huge amounts, but enough to be noticed. Walking to the bakery one day she forgot the reason why she needed to be there, and wound up buying four loaves of bread and did not remember why. Later that week she disappeared and walked all over Pelham Parkway, asking people directions to her apartment complex while standing right in front of it. Both times she sort of snapped back, but slowly and methodically these incidents were more prevalent. As you read her words the disease had started to progress, her mind wandering, her recall limited as you take the next step with her in the journey and hear what happens when someone you love becomes a shell of what they were before.

Ruth

Life is different now. I never know who's coming through that door. One day it could be a fat cow, and another someone tall and thin. I hate all of them. They stare at me, and I just stick out my tongue at them because I know how they feel when they see me.

I do like some of these strangers because they tell me their names when they walk in, and even say "Good morning, Ruthie"…that's me. At least I know who I am. Joyce is great and so is Joan. They are not lazy like the others who sit on their fat duffs and do nothing but wait until their shift is over. My daughter rids me of these people right away. All I have to do is give her the sign and she understands.

Joyce and Joan are my favorite people to care for me. They make great food and even remember NO SALT! They love taking me out, and we sometimes go to Dunkin' Donuts for coffee and some sweet stuff. My daughter treats everyone.

My pills are crushed, and my daughter gives them to me in either yogurt or ice cream twice a day. We go to the stores when we are done, and my daughter buys me new outfits to wear in case I go somewhere special. I love eating, so she and my daughter Marcia constantly bring great meats and other dishes to my apartment so that I never have to go hungry.

Right now I am sitting in my recliner and talking to my daughter as she records my words for all of you to read and understand my journey.

At times I can't remember events, things, or people like I did even yesterday. The world seems to be fading away and getting smaller. At least my world is.

Visions of past events come into my mind but slowly fade away. At times I feel enveloped in a huge black cloud that gets larger and larger and never goes away. Other times there seems to be a thick, foggy mist around my head, covering my eyes and preventing me from seeing the world as it is.

Something has overtaken my thoughts, mind, and thinking skills. But what? I have no idea. Slowly, methodically, and carefully, like a book with its chapters outlined and set in type to be published and printed, my world seems dimmer and my memory all fogged up as this entity takes hold within the recesses of my mind, ready to print out and publish my future.

Sitting on the benches on a nice day is fun. But just the other day I drove to the small diner near where I live for breakfast with my sister, Tova. We talked about different things, and then my daughter walked in and joined us. I spilled the beans at that point, and told them that I knew I had a memory problem, and that things often vanished from my mind, and that I was scared. Even driving there I had made some bad turns and was lucky I was not stopped. We are talking about seeing a neurologist, my primary doctor, and then we played some memory games.

My daughter works with students with learning difficulties, and she was able to see some of the differences in my reading and math skills right away. She found some mental memory tests on Google, and we learned after taking some of them I could not remember dates, days of the week, or even tell time.

Going to the neurologist, I answered all of his questions the following week, but made up some really clever answers when I could not correctly respond.

For example, "Ruthie, what day of the week is it?"

"There are seven," I said. "You pick one!" Smart!

When he asked me what month it was, I said, "Winter…can't you see the snow?"

I needed more tests, and he recommended an MRI, which I knew would not work out since I get nervous in closed spaces. I took the test but never finished it. They were able to learn that I'd had a mini stroke that no one realized, and that might have caused part of the problem. No one said the dreaded "A" word yet. But, in time they would.

Writing things or asking my daughter to record them in this journal helped me to remember. Voices… some are familiar and others are not. How do you live within your own mind each day and not know how to react or respond?

When the doctor asked me to tell him how many quarters in a dollar, I told him four. But, when he asked me to multiply nine times five, I asked for a calculator. Clever! Like a drawing on a magic slate that is there one minute and then gone the next, that is what was happening to me. The worst was yet to come. These are my words and thoughts: My Name Is Ruthie!

Chapter Two

Meet Ruth Swerdloff
Where It All Began

Ruth—*In her own words*

My name is Ruth Swerdloff, and I was born on November 22, 1927, to Max and Fanny Goldberg. Fanny, my mom, was a special person. She spoke five languages and had five children that she loved dearly. Unfortunately, I never really got to know her. She died of pneumonia when I was two, after giving birth to a sixth child.

Having five children and believing that children needed a mother, my dad, Max Jacob Goldberg, decided to find a mother for his five children, but in a very special and old-fashioned way. Fanny had sisters named

Rosie, Tillie, Katie, and Shondina. Each was unique and special in her own way. Shondina was not a very friendly person, and Tillie was a tad spoiled and needed to be taken care of. Rosie was great, but she was married to my Uncle Dave at the time. So, my father decided to choose from the other three sisters, which one Fanny, my mom, would want to bring up her five children.

Three months after her death, my father married Katie. Katie was the only mother that I ever knew, and she was the most amazing, unselfish, smart, and perfect choice to be the mother of five not-so-easy-to-handle kids. There was Tova, my sister, who was ten years older than me. Then there was Irving, Harry, and Kenny. They gave her a really hard time at first because they were old enough to know their real mother, and thought that my dad should have waited before taking a new wife. But, my father was the smartest man in the world, and he made the best and wisest choice, not only in picking a new wife but in business too.

I never knew that Katie was not my real mother until much later. I lived on Southern Boulevard and Tremont Avenue. I went to P.S. 44 and Roosevelt High School. I adored my mom, and I could not understand what the other kids in my family had a problem with until later on when I found out the truth.

22

Growing up I was always closest to my brother Kenny. As the youngest in the family, I can say that I was a tad spoiled and could do no wrong. I loved to dance and wanted to be a Rockette when I grew up. I also loved twirling a baton, and I did become a drum majorette in high school.

I never knew or thought that what would happen to me in later life would ever come to pass. I never heard of Alzheimer's disease, or even dementia. No one in my family ever had a memory problem or anything close to it. As a matter of fact, my mother and father never forgot anything, and neither did my brothers or sister.

Tova was a teacher, and graduated college when she was sixteen years old. You might say she was a genius and could do anything, and could remember things after reading them only once. Kenny went into the army and fought in the Second World War. Irving and Harry were very smart, but due to the Depression and hard times, it was hard to get jobs, and my dad had to figure out a way to help his children make a living when they graduated school.

When my father came to America, he landed on Ellis Island. He brought his family to live in the Bronx, and sold apples on a street corner for a living. Being extremely enterprising, he managed to make enough money to buy a laundromat, and then a cleaning store on 180th Street and Mohegan Avenue. He named the store Arista Cleaners. Arista in school meant the highest, and it was an organization that the smartest kids, who had over ninety averages, were inducted into. Arista Cleaners was the best cleaning store with the highest standards in cleaning, and the best customer service. All of my brothers worked there, and my sister taught in P.S. 67 in the Bronx.

Katie, our mom, was the most amazing woman. She took care of us as if we were her very own children. I know that she even adopted all five of us, but I was too young at the time to know that. When I found out, I was devastated. I was walking home with my cousin from the movies and I realized that I was going to be late. I told her that my mother would be upset, and she said, "Why do you care? She is not your real mother." She proceeded to explain.

I went into our small apartment and into my room, and cried for hours, and hours. I never told anyone that I knew the truth, and I made my cousin swear that she would never tell anyone that she told me. Until the day she died, my mother, Katie, never knew that I found out she was not my real mother. I would never hurt her.

She was so smart and could do anything. She was in a concentration camp in Poland during the First World War and was tortured. They were experimenting with x-rays, and as a result she became sterile and could not have any children. She had other problems because of this. She was practically blind in both eyes due to cataracts, and she was a diabetic, too. She took her insulin and checked her sugar count many times throughout the day.

She could not have her own children and adopted all five of us, and you would never have known that we were not her own kids. She was the most unselfish, caring, and hard-working mother anyone could have. She made sure that we had things even before she did.

When I was in high school she became ill, and I had to stop going to school and take care of her. My brothers and sister worked, and most of the care was on me. But, when they came home from work they were there to support me in every way. I finally did graduate from Roosevelt High School in the Bronx. What a proud day that was for everyone in my family. I became a bookkeeper and worked many jobs before getting married to my true love, Doc.

Life was great until this disease took over. I survived many operations, blood issues, and more. I had three great children and an amazing husband, who took better care of me than anyone can imagine. I miss him every day.

My three children are the best in the world. I taught them responsibility and why getting an education was important. My daughter Fran always got A's in school. I was hardest on her because I knew she could handle the pressures that I put on her. She always did well in school, but if she did not get an A on a test or a perfect grade of 100 percent, I would make her write the entire test over. I felt that she needed to learn from her mistakes. She became a reading and writing specialist and worked in the NYC public schools. Now, she loves writing children's books, articles on many subjects, as well as this book about Alzheimer's.

My daughter Marcia attended Nancy Taylor Business School and worked for ABC News, Xerox Corporation, and now for orthopedic surgeons as their office manager. She has two great children and a lot of grandchildren. She works twelve-hour days and helps many people.

My son, Keith, has three boys and he lives in New Jersey. He tries to come and see me, but it is hard having to work over fifty hours a week and support a family.

I worked as a full-charge bookkeeper for Retail Communications, Master Eagle, and Altman Electronics. I worked in many places when I was younger. I even helped out in my husband's cleaning store on 225th and Laconia Avenue, as did my girls when they were growing up.

I had many friends in my building. One friend that I miss the most is my friend Mary Kaufman. She was like a second sister to me. My daughters and my son loved her like an aunt. When my daughter Marcia would get in trouble she would run away to her apartment one flight up.

There are so many good memories in that building. I had a friend, Flo, whose son was my son's best friend. I have a friend, Sylvia, and another, Shirley, who no longer live here. There are many people that are still here, but they never visit me, even though they might live next door or in the same building. I guess they can't handle what has happened to me. I bet they are afraid that it will happen to them. You never know!

I had four brothers and a sister who are no longer here. I had many sisters-in-law that are no longer here. I have a sister-in-law named Lily who is still here, and I know she calls my children to keep in touch with how

I am doing. They even call her to make sure that she is okay, too.

The rest of my story will be told within the pages of this book.

I am Ruth Swerdloff, and this is my story.

Chapter Three

Before She Knew

Through My Mom's Eyes:
Why Me?

Ruth

Six years ago I was able to drive a car and go shopping by myself. I was even able to eat in a restaurant and have lunch with my children and my sister. I took my own medications. I ran the journal for my organization. I even went around to collect money for ads to promote different businesses in my neighborhood. I had no trouble remembering where I was going and when I was supposed to get there.

Then, all of a sudden I began noticing little things. I could not remember where I put my glasses or my car keys. I could not remember why I walked into a room, or what I was looking for. I began overdosing my meds because I did not recall taking them. This proved to be dangerous and almost fatal.

If that was not bad enough, I could not remember what I had eaten for breakfast, or that I was even hungry. I forgot to get my blood tested each month, thinking I'd had them done the month before. I never remembered calling the doctor for the results, because I did not recall taking them. Worst of all was my ability to drive a car, because my independence was about to come to an abrupt halt. Everything about my life was about to change, and there was nothing that I could do to control or stop it.

All my life I was able to manage what I was going to do and where I was going. I even managed the lives of my children so well that they turned out to do and be exactly what I wanted them to be. A mother could not be more proud.

In May of 2003 I began to realize that I was not really the same person that I was the month before. I did not know that I had had a mini stroke, because not one of my doctors realized it or had me tested for anything like that. Then on the morning of August 25, 2003, I woke up in terrible pain. The pain was in my back, but I could not describe it. My understanding of what had happened was frightening, because I could not begin to explain to anyone why I was in pain or what had caused it. I became frantic and called my sister to come down in the elevator from the 13th floor, because I did not want to scare my daughter.

By the time she called 911 and they came, I was totally incoherent and could barely tell the paramedics the degree of pain that I was in, or where it was located. This was the beginning of the end, as I knew it.

I was transported to the hospital with my daughter and my sister in the ambulance with me. The emergency staff was amazing and did all that they could to try and help find out what had caused the pain. Unfortunately, they were not exactly correct in their diagnosis. They thought that I had an aortic aneurysm, but in reality I had overdosed on my blood thinners and had a bleed out in my left shoulder that had to be addressed before it became fatal. Because of this I could not remain in the trauma center where I was taken; instead, I was taken to another nearby hospital and placed in ICU when I got there. Unfortunately, something happened between hospitals to cause my mental status to deteriorate, and no one wanted to say or admit why in either hospital.

With a breathing tube down my throat, I could not even express to anyone, except with my eyes, how scared I was. My family was not allowed to see me, and I became even more afraid. The following morning I heard the heart surgeon, who I had never met, call my daughter to come to the hospital to sign consent for an operation to identify what was causing the pain in my back, and see if it was indeed a bleed out or, as they originally thought, an aneurism. As a matter of fact, he said it was so serious she could give her consent over the phone. But, she got there in time to see me and tell me that all would be okay before they wheeled me into surgery.

It was not okay. You know how people die and have out of body experiences? Well, I had something like that, but it was hard to describe. I died twice on the table and was revived because my daughter would not allow them to give up on me or allow me to sign a DNR. When I finally came out of surgery and was awake, I realized that I could not speak because of the tubes. I also did not know what had happened, or why.

After two weeks in the hospital, I was sent home, only to return three days later with clots in my legs. At that point the hospital staff placed me in rehab and decided to find out what was really causing the problem.

I knew there was a problem; why couldn't they? I could not work with the speech therapist because I could not remember how to add or subtract simple numbers when she asked me to. I could not even remember what year it was, or the borough that I live in. Simple everyday things were becoming impossible to do and to remember. But, they only got worse when I got home three weeks later.

I realized that I could not stay at home alone any more. My children hired home health aides to assist me for part of the day. I could not take my meds by myself, and my daughter had to prepare them and give them to me twice a day. I could not drive anymore, but refused to allow anyone to sell my car. I hoped in the back of my mind that I would get better and start to be my old self. But, my old self was no longer there. Slowly and deliberately, the mean and terrible web weaved by dementia started to overtake my mind and my body. It creeps in slowly without any warning, and—BAM—it just overtakes you with venom.

I had done everything for everyone in my family. I'd driven my friends where they had to go when they did not have a ride. But, when you have dementia and soon to be Alzheimer's, everyone forgets you, and you no longer exist. You become and feel invisible to yourself and to others. No one remembers to call you to see how you are, or come to visit you.

I really think that people only need you or call when you can do something for them, family included. My nieces and nephews, who I helped throughout their lives, never called me, or even call me now to see how I am. Sometimes when they come to see my daughters, they stop by for a short visit to say hello. But, I really don't remember the last time that happened, and at times I really don't know who they are or why they are in my house.

Well, the worst had not yet hit me until I went to see the neurologist for the first time, and he started to ask me simple questions that I could not answer. I could not tell you where I lived or the state I live in. I could not tell you how many quarters are in a dollar. I was once a full-charge bookkeeper. Now I could not even tell you what I would put in a grocery list or what I wanted for lunch that day.

This became more frightening until I realized that I needed some major help just to get along on a daily basis. It became even worse when I was taken from a restaurant on Mother's Day in 2005 to the hospital because my INR (Blood Clotting: International Normalised Ratio) was too high. I came out of the hospital after a week, a different person.

Imagine being able to take care of yourself somewhat before entering a hospital, and leaving totally helpless and scared. My children realized the difference and got to work to get me some extra help. Unfortunately, if it were up to the staff of the hospital I would have been placed in a nursing home and left to be forgotten with the rest of the people who have this terrifying, humiliating, and awful disease.

I still wonder, in the back of my mind, why the president will not use his power to encourage stem-cell research to find a cure for this and other horrible diseases. I also know that there are drugs out there that will reverse this disease, but we don't have them here in America. I might not be able to tell you what I feel, but watching television, listening to conversations, I know in my own mind that I am being deprived of a full life, because no one seems to want to push it and make these meds available to those of us who need it.

After a while I began to get worse, and going to the neurologist became unnecessary. He told me that he'd done all that he could do, but if my family needed him they could call any time of day and he would help with understanding the disease. He is amazing and has kept his word a thousand times over, and more.

I now have Alzheimer's disease, and there is no cure. I cannot go to the bathroom alone or be alone, because I cannot remember that I even went to the bathroom or have to go. I never remember eating, so I get to eat all day. Of course that could be a plus if I was a big eater before, but I wasn't. I have four strangers that take care of me around the clock, because I cannot be alone. I do not like to be alone, and as the disease progresses so does my behavior. I never used bad language as a child and would punish my children if they did. Now, I can't seem to control it at times, nor can I control my aggressive behaviors or my mood swings. It is not menopause, or hot flashes, it is the disease. I even repeat myself because I cannot remember saying whatever I said in the first place.

I live at home, and my daughter sees me daily to set up my meds, give them to me, and make sure that the aides are taking good care of me. She makes sure that I have plenty of food in the fridge. On Wednesdays and Fridays she walks with me and the aide to go to the stores and buy things. On Thursdays my other daughter comes and we go out to lunch. Last week, I think someone came to see me from my family, but I don't remember whom.

None of my friends call me, and the sad part is

people that live in my building who I've known for over forty years never ring my bell to say hello or see how I am doing. You never know when this disease will get you or anyone in your family. They better hope that their families care about them the way mine cares about me.

My doctor wanted my children to put me in a home, but my daughter, the one with power of attorney and my health proxy, would never allow it. He now says that if not for her I would not even be here. I guess that I am not living the American dream anymore. But, I would rather be on this side of the world than on the other. At least I can still see my children, and I do know who they and my grandchildren are. I might not remember their names, but I know their faces. Oh yeah! Next year I might even get to go to my grandson's bar mitzvah. I really hope I live to see it.

For all of you out there that do not call your mothers and fathers to say I love you and forget all that they did for you, start remembering it, and say thank you. I am so lucky that my children appreciate all that I did, and never once hesitate to make sure that I am all right now.

Maybe there will be a miracle in the near future, and I will be able to remember some of what I lost. If not,

I hope that others will be able to benefit from whatever medical science has to offer. I hope it is soon.

Life will never be the same for me. Many say that you need to have a certain quality of life, or why bother to live? I will let God decide when it is my time to leave this world, not anyone else.

Love,

Ruth Swerdloff

Fran

My mom was a force to be reckoned with. She had her own way of doing things and expected everyone to follow suit. Not easy, to say the least. But it worked for her, and after a while it worked for me, too. Don't get me wrong; my mom was really amazing, loving, and quite distinct in her views and outlook on life. That does not mean she was mean or difficult to live with. It just means that you followed whatever Ruthie would say, making your life much easier and avoiding her lectures and need to have you write out what you might have done differently had you listened to her in the first place. My mom created a schedule for me, which included my activities before and after school and on the weekends. In this way I was never without something to do, and I was lucky if she put in this schedule time to sleep, or even eat. She was tough, smart, and quite opinionated. I guess that's why I turned out the way I did.

Growing up with Ruthie as a mother was a true experience. She was a pure perfectionist, had a definite way of doing things, and she expected you to follow suit in every way. My mom would never allow me or my sister to speak out in public and voice an opinion; she would speak for both of us...or, shall I say, just me. My sister, Marcia, was not introverted, and although I am quite different now, growing up I would let my mother fight my battles and hide behind my sister, who was really quick with her retorts, smart with her sarcastic comments, and braver than me when it came to talking out or speaking back.

School was another area in which I really did excel. I answered in class as long as I knew the right answer, and never ever got in trouble. Well, not until I could not help myself and chanced getting in deep you-know-what when one teacher challenged my integrity. But, that will come later. First, I need to explain more about Ruthie and her relationship with her family.

Chapter Four

Where It All Began

Fran—*as told to me by my mom:*

From the moment she was born, Ruthie was a spitfire, and everyone knew she would be a force to be reckoned with. The youngest of five children, her older brothers would spoil her, give in to her every wish. Blonde, blue-eyed, and spunky, Ruthie from the day she was born knew how to get her own way. Losing her mother at the age of two, she never really realized the transition from Fanny to Katie. Fanny died of pneumonia in childbirth, and Ruthie never realized that my grandfather remarried three months later, since Katie was taking care of the children while my grandfather stayed with Fanny in the hospital praying for the recovery that would not happen.

Her older sister, Tova, resented Katie and would give her a hard time, as did the boys, but not like Tova. She felt she would take charge of Ruthie, and who needed another grown-up telling her what to do. But at twelve, I guess she finally had to realize that if she was going to go to school and become an educator, and she was a great one, Katie would have to care for Ruthie. Once they got to know Katie, or Aunt Katie, they realized that she was a perfect fit for their family.

Grandma Katie had come from Poland when my grandfather went back there and rescued her and her sisters using Poland's underground tunnel. She spent years undergoing some horrific experimental tests at the hands of sadistic and diabolical people hoping to eliminate an entire race of people, and sterilizing young women so they could not have children.

Katie was smart, even though she could not read. She was perceptive and could size up a person just by looking at them. She was a go-to person for advice and help, and helped me deal with my mom when she became difficult.

My mom throughout her life was spoiled in some respects, but my sister and I were not. She was blonde, had the coolest blue eyes, and wanted to become a dance and drum majorette. She entered many competitions and won baton-twirling contests, but because my grandmother needed care at times, she never went any further with her dancing…instead she helped at home.

Graduating from high school took time, because she dropped out for a while to care for Katie. College was not on the horizon for Ruthie. Instead she attended business school and became a full-charge bookkeeper. Numbers and keeping the books was not a hard task for Ruthie. Her skills were almost equal to any accountant's skills, and she enjoyed what she did using the old way of doing things: Adding and subtracting figures by hand, using an old fashioned calculator, but no computers. That was not on Ruthie's desk at home, or at work.

With all of my uncles in the service during WWII, it was up to my mom and my aunt to care for Katie and still have fun. Aunt Tova was a genius. Graduating college at sixteen and getting a teaching job right away made my grandparents so proud. She was able to help with anything that her students could not grasp, and helped Katie, too. Opposites in many ways: Tova was educationally oriented and read books, and Ruthie was more into being social, bookkeeping, and having fun. Ruthie read romance novels, romance magazines, the newspaper, and loved dancing, and singing. She played canasta and mah jong, but never had any other interests. But, before being diagnosed with Alzheimer's, she raised three smart yet different kids!

Being the oldest, and we won't get into age, because that's when my memory fades, I was expected to set the bar and the example for everyone. From the second I entered kindergarten I knew I was in trouble. Even creating the masterpieces that I was told to draw or the designs we made in school, I had to pass not only the teacher's inspection but Ruthie's, too.

Before entering school or being allowed to leave our micro mini apartment on Southern Boulevard in the Bronx, my sister and I had to pass the clothing inspection. My sister was tall, thin, blonde, and really pretty. I was overweight, not so pretty, and tall for my age up until I was ten, and then somehow I forgot to grow past five feet tall. Well, I was at least four feet wide, so I guess that made up for the difference. If one of us—usually me—did not pass the to-definitely-wear inspection, we were sent back to our room to change.

My sister hated to eat breakfast, and I wanted to learn her secret of getting out of eating those awful soft-boiled eggs that my mother and grandmother insisted were healthy. Didn't they ever hear of cholesterol? Well, Grandma would make my eggs hard-boiled, but still

I would rather have had oatmeal, which is still true today. I never eat eggs anymore, and if I do it's only egg whites.

But anyway, Marcia and I went off to school, and our mother followed suit not too long after. Ruthie was the PTA president and her presence was required on a daily basis. The good thing was that no one dared to pick on her two perfect children and, believe me, we were. To get into trouble would have earned the wrath of Ruthie, and you wanted to avoid that at all costs. But, growing up with my mom you learned values; dating was out until you graduated college, and learning to cook…well, no one was allowed near her stove, much less Grandma's. My grandmother owned the kitchen, and when we moved my mother owned hers. My sister loved to bake cupcakes and, of course, eat them. She even made puddings and could pig out without gaining weight. All I had to do was watch her making them, and I would put on forty pounds.

My mom was a firm believer in not allowing anyone to have the summer off from work or responsibility. So, my sister and I had a choice: Advancing in summer school, or working as a camp counselor.

This is not about me, my sister, or my brother; this is about an amazing woman whose voice and thoughts were silenced by a deadly illness, and if she could speak to you right now these are the thoughts she wrote in her journal from the moment she realized something had changed. 2004: when it started to change and sink in!

Chapter Five

Before Alzheimer's There Was Ruthie

Ruth—*In her own words*

How do you say goodbye when you are still here? How do you say goodbye when you know that your thoughts, desires, and wishes can no longer be heard? What happens when all that is left of you is a human shell? Sitting in my car in front of a local diner, I just sat there staring out of the window, wondering what I was supposed to do and where I was going. Looking at the keys in my hand, they seemed like a foreign object, and the ignition of the car looked like something you put something into, but I had no idea what. It took me a while to focus and then realize what I had to do.

For weeks now I had been forgetting where I put my keys, where I was going, or even the names of people that I had known for years. I just thought it was because I had pressing problems on my mind, things cluttering my thoughts, and I never realized that I was losing memory. Not realizing the gravity of the situation but being someone that liked to have a handle on everything, I decided to keep a log of these episodes, or at least try to, but not say anything to anyone.

Days would pass and I would be fine. Maybe I would forget to shut off a light, lock the door, or even pay for bread in the bakery. Maybe I would even forget where I put my eyeglasses, but not until I made one grave mistake while driving home from the doctor's office one afternoon did I realize that something might be wrong.

My name is Ruthie, and this is my story before I became something or someone else. Before, I could remember everything; add columns in my head, do bookkeeping for many companies, travel by bus to the city, and even drive to my son's house to take care of his three young boys. Before, I could drive to Atlantic City, pick up friends to go to a show, and chauffeur my daughter to parties and to the homes of friends. Before, I could do anything.

Now, I tend to forget, get tired easily, and often cannot remember what I started to do, no less finish it. But, on that fateful day I was driving home and decided to take a shortcut down a one-way street. I passed through four red lights, made a U turn in the wrong spot, and was finally stopped by three police cars. You might say I was surrounded. I had no idea what I had done wrong.

One incident that I wrote in this journal stayed with me until it left my mind completely. You see, Alzheimer's is cruel. It does not ask your permission to come into your brain, it just does. It roams around, finds its way, and destroys all of your thought processes in its own timely fashion. I remember sitting in a diner with my daughter having breakfast and telling her that I had trouble adding and subtracting numbers. We began practicing to try and sharpen my skills. It did help for a while. At times I would forget names of family members, so my two daughters created albums of pictures, and with my help we labeled them and went over them every day. After all, if someone did come to visit it would be nice if I remembered his or her name. Added in, there was one incident that really started to bring out what was happening to me at home. I went out for a while and forgot to lock my door. I took what little money that I had in my wallet and went down the street to buy a loaf of bread. That in of itself is okay, you might say, but what I remember doing next was dangerous. I flagged down a car that was going my way—or at least I thought the driver was headed for my building, which was just about a block from the bakery—and offered to pay the driver to take me home. You see, my legs hurt and I was having trouble walking up the huge hill in front of my building, or even up the driveway to my building's entrance.

I also forgot that the home health aide was coming. When she arrived, she claimed the door was opened, so she went into my apartment and called my daughter, who came straight home, finding me sitting in my favorite chair and reminding me of why what I did was dangerous. Also making me realize that I might need more help to monitor my movements, and make sure that I was safe and did not do this again. No one yelled or screamed. Everyone explained why going into a car with a stranger could have been tragic.

Fran

This was to be the first of many incidents that led my sister and me to believe that something was wrong and needed to be addressed. As a result of this incident and several others, my mom agreed to see my aunt's neurologist and have the dreaded MRI. She barely made it through the test, having a case of claustrophobia, and demanded the test be over. But, the results of a CAT scan taken on a different day showed she'd had a mini stroke that no one had even realized.

Unfortunately, because no one knew if she was taking her Coumadin on time or even overdosing on it, she took more than the required dosage on a daily basis. Rarely remembering to go for her INR—a blood test to find out if her blood was too thin or too thick—unless I went with her, she claimed to have had it done, but it was apparent that I needed to check up on her, and I did. Making weekly and then bi-weekly appointments to make sure her INR levels were within the right range, it slowly became necessary for me to administer the right dosages each day.

In August of 2003 my family's life drastically changed. On August 25 of that year, my mom got sick. She woke up with a sharp pain in her back and could hardly breathe. She called my aunt and told her to come down to her apartment and not to call my sister, or me. She wanted to handle this without worrying either one of us. However, this was not to be.

My aunt called 911 and they responded to the call, but insisted that one of her children be present when they did the initial exam and assessment. I was and still am the only one who knows what meds my mom takes, how often, and the dosage. After dealing with the preliminary issues and arriving at the hospital, the staff immediately addressed my mother's issues and concerns. They did numerous tests to find out what had caused her problem. From what she was saying, it sounded like she did not remember taking her blood thinner medicine and had overdosed on it by accident. She had always been very careful with her Coumadin.

My mom took Coumadin because she had experienced clots in her legs, arms, and lungs, and she took this medication to prevent these clots and to reduce her risk of stroke or heart attack. Unfortunately, this took a great toll on her when she became unable to deal with the dosages and the times to take it. Forgetting could result in her blood being too thick, and taking too much would make her blood too thin.

Mom had been forgetting to take the Coumadin, and was forgetting a lot more, too. This only got worse as time went on.

From this hospital, she was taken by ambulance to another one, where they thought they could address what they believed was an aortic aneurysm. However, this was incorrect.

The following morning I received a call from the heart surgeon in charge of my mom's case, asking permission to operate to find the problem before it was too late. Of course, I did not hesitate and allowed him to save her life. Fortunately, I got there just in time to see her before surgery. This was the last time she would sound lucid or clear for a very long time.

She came out of the operation with many more problems. She had died twice on the table and had to be revived. (I was told this later on.) She began to slur her words, and she did not understand what was happening around her. The physical operation was a success, but her mental capacity for dealing with things and understanding what was happening around her were greatly diminished.

When she finally came home from the hospital two weeks later, she had to reenter it the next day due to complications that no one realized when she was discharged. Because of four more stays in the hospital, my family and I noticed that her ability to process information and deal with daily situations had been compromised by the surgery and the anesthesia that was given. She even realized that she could no longer remain alone for any long period of time.

Due to all of the stays in the hospital and many other factors that changed her ability to care for herself, we were forced to find help for her by enlisting VNS—Visiting Nurse Service—to find aides to care for her the right way. Unfortunately, this turned out to be costly to my family and me. I had to change my lifestyle and my way of living, which no one seemed to care about. I had to retire from teaching early and find other interests that I could pursue at home. One, of course, was writing books, and the other short stories. I have even tried to publicize the fact that I am writing a book about Alzheimer's as a resource for other families to be able to learn more about this illness, and to get the help and care they need for a loved one.

The only problem is that no one realizes that as the person who has to deal with nurses, doctors, home care agencies, and home care providers, you still need to take time for yourself and have some kind of life. I have been nowhere for the last seven years, since my mom was diagnosed with this awful illness. She is getting much worse, and now rather than make her presence known, she just stares all day while sitting on a chair in front of her television. Although the aides do try and sometimes succeed in taking her out in her wheelchair to get some air and possibly run into an old friend who might stop and say hello, she often rebels and refuses to leave her chair. It seems like it is her safety net, and she is afraid of anything that is different or a change in general.

It is really hard to remain calm and neutral when it comes to other family members that go away on vacation and do not check and see how my mom is, or if there is something that I might have planned or need to do. They usually plan their flights or trips, and tell me about them when they have their trips finalized. This gets me quite upset, and I often get into it with the other person. I try to explain that there are times that I would like to just do something during the day, or even stay over in a hotel with my husband for the night. The home health aides are not allowed to give my mom her meds. I have to give them to her twice a day. I can put them together once in a while in the morning, but the pill she takes to stay calm should not be given in a double dose in the morning. She would be too calm and possibly sleep through the day, making it hard for the day aide to feed her.

People forget that caregivers might actually do other things during the day. So, when I state that I am busy writing an article for a magazine, or just for one of my books, or to post on one of the many internet sites that I belong to, people often say, "What are you busy with? You don't work." I work from home, and probably get more done in a day than they do working in an office. I never put anyone down and I respect whatever others do.

I worked for over thirty-six years in the New York City public schools, and I miss working with the students in reading and writing every day. I had fun teaching my writing classes, and working with students in reading, and teaching the classics was not only fun, but it was also very rewarding.

Caregivers are people, too, and not just people who provide time and care for a person who is ill. Others need to understand that the caregiver needs time to regroup and regenerate him or herself, and take time to feel.

The care became more difficult every day. Seeing my mom withering away not just her mind, but her spirit and her soul, was not easy. Yet in the back of my mind, although many would think I was wrong, I needed to remember my promise.

My mom spent a lot of time in the hospital, and one morning I arrived to check on her and speak with the head nurse to learn that she, without my permission, had asked a representative of a nursing home to see me about admitting my mom that day rather than taking her home. It took me a while to calm down and I had to keep my mouth in check. When I did meet with the representative, I learned that the head nurse had taken it upon herself to call and state that I would sign.

Fuming, angry, and not about to let this pass for one second, I made it clear that it would never happen, and I proceeded to file a complaint with the administration. If that was not enough, I decided to deal with this in my own special way. I visited about twenty different homes throughout the Bronx, and even one supposedly state-of-the-art one (not so) in Riverdale to see what they had to offer someone with Alzheimer's. I wanted to learn what kind of life she would have in a care facility.

At one care facility that was near where we lived, the rooms were dark and dingy and had an awful odor. When we went to see the recreation center, one of the residents came up to the person taking us around, and the worker pushed the patient away and made her stand in the corner until she was ready to deal with her.

I could not believe this abuse in front of anyone, much less anyone wanting to leave a loved one there. And you can be sure I said that out loud.

I went to another one where the patients were drugged, not responsive, and in wheelchairs in the hall while the aide drank coffee, sat and talked on her cell phone, and laughed at them. The families of these people, or anyone who places a loved one in a home, had better do their homework. They need to make sure they visit at least once, if not twice, a day, and find out what is being done to create a somewhat normal life for their loved one.

Sometimes the workers do not even care if their patients eat, as long as they are quiet and not bothering them. It's so sad! When the hospital officials told me that I had to meet with them about placing my mom in a home, I threw twenty brochures on the table and asked each one to take one and decide if they would feel safe there. Then, I called my lawyer in front of them, and they relented.

My mom never gave up in her own way, yet there were times I became frustrated because there was no one to give me time to do anything. The aides would take her for nails and for her hair, but I had to go with them. When something happened in the middle of the night,

Fran Lewis

I had to go to the hospital in the ambulance with the aide, my mother, and the paramedics. I have to say the New York Fire Department and EMT's were exemplary. They came right away and handled everything, making the transition to the hospital smooth. But, each time my mom arrived at the hospital, the ER doctors would say, "Why not let her go?" Even her own doctor wondered why I would not sign a DNR to let her go.

I realized that at times they tried to make a solid case, but to me, that was murder. I believed when God wanted her, that's when she would go, and it was not up to the doctors; It was up to Him!

Ruth

You won't believe it, but today was really hot and the aide decided to take me out in my wheelchair. It was 105 degrees, but the home health aide decided to take me out in my wheelchair in order to go shopping and buy something for her daughter. I did not want to go out and I, at this time, couldn't express myself, but she was determined to go out. So, I had no choice, and if my daughter learns about this the aide will definitely be eliminated from my life.

Getting to the store I refused to go in, and instead of returning home to my apartment or bringing me in anyway, she left me sitting in my chair in the sweltering heat. When she came out, I was gone. She had no idea where I was, but she had bought several items for her daughter. Returning to my apartment, how could she think I would be there?

Fran

As the aide walked up to my apartment, she stated, "I LOST YOUR MOTHER!" I replied, "Just how did you manage to lose someone in a wheelchair who cannot walk or wheel herself, and why didn't you call the police?"

With her seeming to not comprehend what I said, I told her to disappear from my sight, and I proceeded to go down to the store and questioned the guard, who did see my mom outside but never thought to do anything when someone odd, he said, wheeled her away. He did not think she might have been kidnapped, or worse. It's a sad world when no one takes notice and tries to help someone in need.

But, things got worse before getting better, and the aide trekked down to the store, at which point I stopped a police car and relayed what I knew about my mom's disappearance. Calling many different emergency rooms and questioning the aide, who'd materialized but was warned to keep out of my reach, we learned that mom was taken to a local hospital and was being treated for heat stroke and dehydration. Thanking the police and leaving them to deal with the aide and her agency, I headed with my husband to the hospital to learn that someone had actually called an ambulance and was caring for her. Seeing this man I was not sure that I would have trusted him, but he came closer and whispered, "I told them I was her son and you are my sister. Otherwise they would not have admitted her and I could not stay." I had tears in my eyes. I could not believe that this compassionate man named John cared so deeply for my mother.

I had a cold and did not feel great, but my mom was still my mom, and her sense of humor came through when she saw me. Her exact words were, "It's about time you got here. What took you so long?" I cracked up laughing. I told her she was missing and I had to go to the lost and found to find her. "HA HA, not funny," but she didn't mean that.

John stayed with me the entire time until I had to go home and deal with a replacement aide. My mom was going to be there for a while, so they told us to leave and come back when she was fully hydrated. We drove John home, and my husband and I gave him something for remaining with her and saving her life. He was touched and appreciated the fact that we appreciated his help, and we thanked him. I often wonder what happened to him, but I can tell you the aide was fired and she, I hope, would never care for another patient again.

The agency realized that they had made a big mistake and other actions were taken. Once again someone dared to say, "It would be easier if you put her in a home, and then you would not have to worry about this happening again." The ire in my voice and the rise in octave told them that covering up their mistake and that of the aide would not cut it. Placing mom in a home would make me worry even more, since there were few homes where the aides and nurses really cared. Not every home is abusive or poorly run, but even the best ones had some questionable methods of care. Once again: A daughter's promise never faltered, or broken.

Chapter Six

Why Me?

Ruth—*As dictated to Fran*

The harsh truth sets in and the family begins to face the inevitable, along with ME!

My name is Ruth Swerdloff, and WHY ME? I spend my days sitting in a chair and just staring at the screen on my television set and letting the world go by. I am a vibrant and energetic woman; at least I used to be.

Everyone invites guests to their homes for dinner, or just to talk. But, some guests overstay their welcome and others are just plain annoying. Uninvited guests can be escorted out and asked to leave, hopefully never to return. One guest made his way inside my home, namely my mind and brain, uninvited, and refuses to leave. No matter how many times I beg, it's all going to deaf ears.

I realized that something was wrong when I decided to go to the bakery to buy two loaves of bread. Standing in line, I became impatient and demanded that I be served before anyone else. I did not care that there were at least ten other people there before me. I refused to be ignored and left waiting. I became irritable, angry, and started yelling, and demanded that they give me two loaves of bread because I was being starved at home and no one would feed me. Of course that was not true, but I felt that this might help get me served faster. Besides, for a short moment I actually believed what I was saying.

I got cold stares, stares of disbelief, anger, and definitely strange looks, as well as many mumbling under their breath thinking I was deaf and could not hear their harsh words.

"I'm all alone," I kept saying," and I am starving. They took all of my money and refuse to feed me. They are supposed to care for me. Look at me. I need food."

Realizing that I was making a scene, the owner packed up two loaves of bread and some rolls and quietly escorted me to the door, hoping that I would just disappear or go home.

Walking home, I hoped in the right direction, I stopped a stranger, getting into her car, and asked her for a ride home. I told her my legs hurt and I really could not walk up the huge hill to my building. This was not smart, as my daughter told me later that day. But, all I wanted was to get home.

While I was dealing with the bakery people and getting food, my daughter received a frantic phone call from my home health aide, who'd arrived and found the door to my apartment unlocked and opened. No one knew where I was until I sauntered in about thirty minutes later.

My name is Ruthie. Before I knew it, Alzheimer's began taking over my brain, like an evil demon preying on my mind and destroying my thoughts. Slowly, methodically, and well planned out, this horrific disease destroys you as a person, your ability to speak and communicate, and takes away your dignity. Before I knew it, I was someone else.

Behaviors change when you have this disease. From a calm, understanding, and kind person, I became aggressive, rude, violent, and nasty at times. I could not help myself. Before I would chauffeur all of my friends to meetings, games, and luncheons. I would play canasta, bridge, and even poker, and I had fun going to the movies and eating out with my family and friends. Having other people take care of my daily needs was embarrassing at first, and later I never really knew. Things changed rapidly. But, first let me tell you about me before this disease won!

Dear God:

Why Me? I wonder every day, although I really do not understand anything at all anymore. Why did this happen and is still happening to me? I can no longer understand what anyone says to me. I can no longer understand what is expected of me. Why ME? Why did I get this awful and humiliating disease? I know that we are not supposed to question why bad things happen to us, but why does my family have to be destroyed because of this, too?

I have always believed in God, and somewhere in me I probably still do. But, I have the last stages of Alzheimer's and can do nothing without the total help of another person who understands my problems and can help me to exist. I made my daughter promise me that she would never place me in a nursing home, and she has kept her word, although the battle with the home care agency still hangs over her head every year, and at the present time, I know that she is strong and will prevail on my behalf.

I have gone through so much in the last sixteen years that it is amazing that I am still here. I have a strong spirit, and hope that the cure is just minutes away and I will be back to myself. I know that is wishful thinking, and I also know that it is not a reality. Actually, I really do not know anything of the sort. I cannot understand what has been written here, but if I could this is what I would tell you about my life, and I hope everyone will understand the power of love, understanding, and most of all God.

Chapter Seven

Miracles Do Happen

Through the eyes of "Miracle"—*Ruthie's stuffed animal*

Read my story and really listen to my words. You will feel what I went through, and you will understand that just when you think all is lost, the most amazing things can happen.

Miracle's story is dedicated to my mom, who is, and always will be, the strength and guiding force in our family.

My name is Miracle, and I am a white stuffed animal that was given to someone special in 1994. I was named Miracle because the person that I was given to is alive because of a series of miraculous things that happened to her. I can honestly say that it is really hard to believe all that she went through, and her fight to survive. No one believed in her, and no one believed that she would pray, fight, and struggle to stay alive and never give up. You decide whether it was a miracle or, as I believe, divine intervention and a lot of prayer too.

It started way back in 1993, when she was diagnosed with serious blood clots in her lungs. These clots covered the inside of her chest cavity. X-rays showed nothing but black patches and black spots covering her heart and lungs. What to do? All but one doctor had no clue and no solutions to save this brave woman, who had already survived so many things her life. In comes this one doctor with what he hoped was the solution. He had read about two doctors at the University of California, San Diego (UCSD), who had invented and created a procedure so far advanced and so technical that only they could perform the surgery with any success.

The diagnosis was grim, and the family and the patient had no idea what was in store for her. Realizing how ill she was, she had no choice but to agree to the surgery and go to California. Problem number one was to find a mode of transportation, other than commercial airlines. This was costly and had to be paid outright by the family. I could feel the tension in the family members, and I knew that somehow this first hurdle would be met.

Her daughter contacted several private airlines that handled cases in which the patient needed medical care. Unfortunately, even though the airline had a good reputation, it did not live up to what it promised. When she contacted the owner of this airline, he promised her a Leer Jet, equipped with medical personnel and equipment for her mom's survival, and food, water, and a bathroom in order to keep her comfortable during the six-hour trip.

I was getting excited because I knew she would be there soon, and I hoped to meet her so that she could feel how much I wanted her to survive. But, this did not happen. Hurdle one was paying for the plane, and her brother did that. However, hurdle two was convincing one of the children to go along with her and miss work for over a month. I guess daughter number one, the oldest, was unanimously chosen.

As they traveled to Teterboro Airport for their flight to UCSD, no one could foresee hurdle number three, which could have cost everyone, including the pilots and the paramedic, their lives. This is when I knew that her daughter believed in miracles, God, and prayer.

The surgery she required would take over twenty hours, and it was doubtful, even if the flight went smoothly, that she would even survive. The day of the flight there was a major snowstorm. Over nine inches of snow had fallen on the ground when they arrived at the airport. But, this was not going to stop them from flying. The trip would be embedded in the minds of her daughter and her forever.

This is when the nightmare began and her faith in God took over. As the plane lifted off the runway, the pilots looked disturbed about something and said nothing to their passengers. About an hour later her daughter questioned them as to why they were checking their navigation equipment and looking at maps. As she insisted on a response, they said the steering mechanism was faulty, and the plane would not be landing in the scheduled place. They decided to land in Alabama and not New Mexico to refuel.

What happened next was really awful, or just plain funny. When Fran, her daughter, asked where the bathroom was on the plane, they handed her a bedpan. With no doors or any enclosure, the poor thing had to cover herself with blankets in order to get some privacy. When finished, she had the paramedic discard the contents.

If that was not enough, there was no food or water on the airplane. For $12,500 you would think that the airline would provide food. At the first stop, her daughter phoned her brother, who she instructed to stop the payment on the check. She then proceeded to deal with the airlines and make them aware of her complaints and concerns for her mom's survival.

As the pilot deplaned, I guess he did not realize that the door was so heavy and his hand got caught in the door and he broke it. Although this was quite painful and maybe someone's way of saying you should be more considerate and compassionate of others, this delayed their flight for over three hours.

Due to the weather and the gravity of the situation, a new pilot was requested who would be able to fly them to UCSD. However, the paramedic had other ideas and told her daughter he would pay for a ticket on a commercial airline to get rid of her accompanying her mom. It would never happen.

At this point Fran requested a private room to pray and deal with her feelings. She started to speak to God and to her Father in Heaven, and felt a chill throughout her entire body. She knew right then and there that everything would be fine. She just felt it and believed it, and felt her strength come back, and she was renewed.

After sixteen and a half hours of ups and downs at different airports, they arrived in California and were met by an ambulance, which took them to the hospital. This is where the miracle of God took over, and her prayers were finally heard. The doctors met both Fran and her mom at the entrance of the hospital and quickly whisked her mom away for medical assessment. They sent Fran to her hotel, only to call her to come back not four hours later. When she arrived, she was taken to a private floor, where her mom was declared more than critical, and they felt that she needed to call her family in New York to either come or be ready for the worst.

Looking into the faces of these unknown doctors and hospital staff, Fran said, "I did not come sixteen or more hours for a gloom and doom result. I did not travel on a plane that almost crashed for you to tell me she was not going to survive. Find a way to raise her blood pressure and fix the problem. I will not let another set of doctors give up like the ones in New York did with my dad."

With looks of disbelief they asked her to sign several forms so that they could administer the treatment they felt might work. About one hour later, they told her she would be able to have the surgery the next day, but they were doubtful of the outcome.

Miracles do happen when you believe they will. Miracles do happen when you feel and believe in the people that can really make it happen. For whatever reason, Fran felt the strength, the compassion, and the understanding that these doctors had for her mom, and she knew that if she prayed real hard and had faith, she would survive…and she did.

This is where I come in. When her mom was taken to critical ICU, they put me on her nightstand to watch over her. The doctors felt that since she had come so far, she might make it. Her daughter named me Miracle, because she said that the name fit. I am a soft white cuddly bear and have a soft middle. When people look at me, they feel the warmth and comfort that I exude. I love Ruth and I love her family. They are a rare group of people who have sacrificed a lot to keep her alive. Few families would give up their time at work for months to come to a place where they know no one, and had to spend their time all alone.

You could feel the support and the love in the air all around us. At times in the waiting room, things often became stressful and bleak. Everyone there had a loved one that was critical, and everyone there was hopeful for the survival of his or her loved one. There were people there that realized that the outcome might not be positive. However, no one would give up and everyone, with me in Fran's arms, would go to the hospital's chapel and pray. If they did not go to the chapel, they would form a circle in the waiting room, and sing and chant and pray together. Strangers from different countries of the world came together to speak to God and let Him hear our prayers. And He did!

When her mom finally did wake up, and they knew she was going to survive, they moved her to another part of the hospital. This is when everyone got to know the real Ruth and just what a force she was to be reckoned with. Her strong personality and her strong will came through, even though she could not speak. She used a slate to write down what she wanted to express. With a feeding tube preventing her from getting real food, she expressed the need for ice cream or yogurt. She wrote what flavors she wanted, and began yelling in her own way with the tube and writing that she demanded these foods, NOW! It was funny to see her doing this.

Fran explained, and so did the nurse, that it would be a few more days before she would be able to eat. She was not listening. So, when she wrote, "In that case, what would you do?" Fran told her she could get her a hairdresser and someone to do her nails. The rest was out of her hands.

As a result of the care in UCSD, and the dedication of the nurses and the doctors, she brought me home two months later and gave me the place of honor on her bed on the pillow next to hers. Although she rarely ever sleeps in her bed, I am always by her side, her Miracle.

Miracle is now with my daughter, Fran, giving her the same hope and joy that it gave me.

Fran

Unfortunately, in 2003 what some would think was another miracle happened, while most would disagree. This time my mom was taken by ambulance to a hospital that was not skilled to meet her medical needs, and although she had survived major heart surgery and more, she did not come out as strong and physically fit this time. Her mind was not as sharp, and her thinking was clouded. She could no longer understand simple directions, nor could she do basic daily life activities, like adding or subtracting or turning on a television. She even had problems using the phone and understanding what people were telling her.

Miracles happen, and then you need to pray for one more and hope that you have not run out of the amount you have been allotted. My mom really needs a big one, and she deserves it. Although her voice cannot be heard to defend what she needs, her family's voice will be loud and clear. She is in the last stages of Alzheimer's and has home health aides that cherish her and are trained to handle her needs. I am a firm believer that it is up to God to decide when a life is over, and not to doctors or anyone else. Her wishes were respected by her family to keep her home and not in a nursing home with strangers. But, we need to pray that the agency that provides care does not take it away and send people who are new and are totally not trained to understand my mom and her needs. I have been praying and hoping that someone will be able to help me find a way to make sure that this does not happen.

I grew up going to temple every week with my grandfather. He instilled in me many beliefs, and taught me to understand our religion and heritage. I studied the Torah with him at home and in temple on Saturdays, and later with my friends on Friday and Saturday mornings. I never rode in cars or elevators on the Sabbath, and I walked with my friends on Saturday afternoons. I grew up learning about the different beliefs of my people and the differences between Orthodox, Conservative, and Reformed. I loved studying the Five

Books of Moses, and I enjoyed going to temple and hearing the rabbi's speech.

I miss those times, and I still have the same strong beliefs that I did as a child. I guess when my father died in 1987, I became very skeptical because the doctors could have but did nothing to save him. They kept insisting that my mom disconnect the life support systems, which would give him a chance to come back to us. I know that when you speak to someone in a coma they are supposed to hear you. I cannot say that for sure.

God decides our fate and how long we have on this earth. I know that being a good person and trying to help others is something that I always try to do. I think I ran out of miracles after this last one!

Ruth—*Life as I see it now*

Ruth Swerdloff's words if she could tell you what her days are like.

My day started when I opened my eyes and found myself sleeping in my chair. I tried to get up, but someone stopped me. I jumped at the sound of the person's voice and became scared and frightened. I started to scream, "Get out of my house! Why are you here?" Then, I used some profanities and started saying things to this person and telling them to leave. Finally, I cried so hard and so uncontrollably that I began to shake. All the while this person was trying to calm me down and told me, "Ruth, everything will be okay. It's me, Joan...you know me. I love you."

Joan stood in front of me, and I really didn't know her name, or anyone else's for that matter, but I did know her face. Then, my day began with her taking me to the bathroom and helping me get cleaned up. I smelled something and realized that I had soiled my diaper, and I was not capable of changing it. I tried to tell her that, but it came out like, "I know you did it, I think so too, just do it. Don't you remember?" That seemed to be what I said a lot of the time. I didn't know why.

After getting me cleaned up, she took me into another place and gave me food. I had no idea what she was giving me. I looked at it and she said it was called oatmeal. It could have been anything, and I would not have known it. She could have given me dog food or worse and I would have still eaten it if I felt hungry. The trouble was....

I can't remember what I was going to say. I started to tell her the oatmeal was no good, but I could not tell her why. I just stared out into space and forgot that I was even eating anything at all. She asked me what was no good, and I began shouting, "NO GOOD, NO GOOD, NO GOOD," and threw the spoon at her and on the floor. I thought she was about to say something when my daughter walked in and saw what had happened. She looked at me covered in oatmeal and the food all over the floor, and asked Joan what had caused me go get so agitated. I was trying to say that the oatmeal was too hot, but I could not remember what hot meant, or that it needed some sugar because I liked things sweeter.

My daughter looked at me and just smiled. I knew everything would be okay because she was there. She came to give me something that looked like a lot of things, but I didn't know why I had to take them to stay alive. Some looked like candy, some looked like round things, and the rest looked like mush. She called it my medicine, and said that I needed to take these things in order to be okay. I just spit them all out and yelled, "NO!"

Then all of a sudden something strange that had never happened before really put me over the edge. I started to curse and use all kinds of bad words, and could not stop myself. I kept telling whoever the fat lady was that was in my house to "Get out, you fat thing, and never come back!"

She stayed calm. She just said, "Ruthie, we all love you, it will be okay."

I just glared at her in total horror and started to try and leave. "I am not staying here with you. You can't make me. I hate you!" I was ranting like a crazy lady and could not stop. All of a sudden someone else came, and both of them just looked at me and did not know whether to laugh or cry. I didn't know what I'd done.

I went back to sleep on my chair and let them worry about what to do. When I woke up again I did not remember what had happened before, but I knew something in me had changed. I began talking funny and sounded like something out of a horror movie. I started yelling, "WOO, WOO, WOO, WOO," and waving my arms as if I was possessed. I started smiling strangely. I heard the two of them say that I sounded like I thought I was a different person trying out different voices. I had no idea what they were talking about.

I started to pretend I was dancing and said, "I want to float and fly over there with the birds. Don't you see them?" Then I said, "I want to go over there and eat, and eat all of you." I could not control my words or what I was saying.

I became so out of control that Joan had to call my neighbor and my daughter to stop me from yelling and screaming. All I kept saying was, "Don't you remember? Leave me alone! Get out of here, and stop trying to kill me!" I started to speak but no one knew who it was. I sounded like three different people, and they thought I was going crazy.

Throughout the day the same things happened until I got an extra dose of Risperdal to help control my outbursts and calm me down. Even the doctor did not know what to say when they called him. His words were, "That is the disease progressing, and get used to it." Get used to what? Not knowing who you are or who anyone else happens to be? I did not even know my own daughter, who was standing next to me and trying her best to stay calm for my benefit.

What happened next was earthshaking, and even worse. All of a sudden the aide saw something brown and awful on the carpet when she went to help me to the table to eat something. It went down my legs, and I could not control or stop it from coming. It looked like a river of dark chocolate. She just shook her head and took me to the bathroom and did her best not to get upset. The rug, her shoes, the carpet, and of course me were one big mess and smell. I started to cry, because

I knew that I'd done something bad. I said, "I am bad, I am sorry. Don't yell at me." Of course, no one did.

When it got dark I got scared because I couldn't tell the difference between day and night. I just sat in my chair and watched whatever was on that thing in front of me. Sometimes I talked to the people on that thing and started yelling at them. If I saw someone on it hurting someone, I thought it was really happening. If I saw something I didn't like, I started screaming and yelling for someone to change it.

Life has not been the same for me for over six years. It will probably only get worse. My children told me I am going to be eighty-one years old on Thanksgiving day. I don't even know what that means. All I said when they told me I was going to my son's for that day is "okay." Then, "I want my son, I want him now. No one else cares about me. Just him." I guess I say that because he is always working, and I really never see him except when I imagine it in my dreams.

I see a lot of people in my dreams. I see my husband and my sister who are not here anymore. I see my brothers, too. I talk to myself, and sometimes I even talk to pictures on the piano and to that thing in front of me. When am I going to be myself again? When is anyone going to be able to help me? I think the answer is NEVER!

How would you like to live each day like this?

Fran

I wrote this book so that everyone who has ever had to deal with a parent with this illness understands what the person is going through. My mom is so special, and so many of her friends and family members have forgotten all of the things that she did for them until her illness caused her to become so dependent on other people.

Chapter Eight

The Beginning of the End

Ruth

In July of this year everything in my life changed. Rather than go through the events on a daily basis, I will tell you about them as I remember them.

It started with an eye doctor's appointment and a brain MRI. I found out that I had had a mini stroke and did not even know it. No one picked it up, not even my doctors, nor did the eye doctor that suggested I take the MRI. I complained of headaches and found out that I had this mini stroke. It was at that point that I began to realize that I could not recall simple events, dates, or people's names without having to stop and think. I even had trouble remembering whether I had taken my medications. I had trouble driving and wound up on a one-way street without even realizing what I had done.

In August things only got worse. On August 25 I woke up with a terrible pain in my back. I called my sister Tova. She came down to my apartment. I could not explain what was wrong with me and she called my daughter to come down, too. By the time the paramedics came I was totally incoherent and could not express myself at all. I could not even remember where my medication bottles were, and my daughter had to go searching for them. Luckily, she knew what I was taking and was able to give the EMT's accurate information.

But, things only got worse. I was taken to the hospital and diagnosed with a heart problem. That was not the case. It was really something totally different, but no one knew this from all of the tests taken. They saw what they thought was an aortic aneurysm, but in reality was a bleed out in my left shoulder. I had overdosed on Coumadin and did not realize it. I did not remember taking my meds.

I wound up in surgery and I had to be revived twice while on the table. When I came home I was not the same person I was before. My memory was a little worse, but not so bad that I was unaware of what was happening to me. But, I could not remember taking my meds, and my daughter decided she would help me remember it daily and make sure I took the correct dosage of all of my meds when I was supposed to.

I was in the hospital on and off the entire month for blood clots and rehab. The agency that was supposed to send a nurse to help me always forgot. I had to have another surgery, but I was awake this time. The doctor said he'd made a mistake and it resulted in my needing a second surgery on my leg to clean out an infection that would not go away. When I came home this time, the doctor made sure that the agency knew to send the nurse twice a day to clean out my wound. But, this time my daughter did not take any chances, and she went to a different health care provider and a different home health care agency.

Throughout the rest of 2003 and into the start of the next year I was able to live alone and take care of myself. I even started to drive again. Then one day I took my daughter to the doctor and I had a rude awakening. I came to an intersection and drove past three red lights and went down a one-way street, telling her I knew what I was doing. Two very unfriendly police officers that wanted to give me at least eight tickets for at least eight serious violations stopped me. But, by the time my daughter explained my problem and my state of confusion, we were lucky they let me go with a warning.

It was when I got home that day that my daughter told me to consider not driving any more. I would not hear of it. But, a month later the same thing happened and she and my other daughter hid the two sets of keys to the car and refused to let me drive anywhere. They told me to take Access A Ride or a car service to get where I had to go if someone was not around to drive me. I was livid, but I had no choice.

In June of that year, my daughter Marcia sold my car in order to make sure that I did not call a locksmith to make a new set of keys.

It was in August of 2004 that I realized that I needed some help at home, and thus the beginning of the real end of my independence and freedom. My daughters hired an aide to help me four hours a day, five days a week. It cost a fortune. But, they did not care. They wanted me safe and taken care of. However, the first ten aides were awful, and the three agencies were even worse. In December of 2004 was when my daughter Fran called VNS and asked for Partner's In Care. What a smart and great move that was.

Fran Lewis

I began to realize that my memory was really starting to fail, and it had nothing to do with getting older. I forgot what I ate for breakfast and did not remember even eating. I forgot to get my blood draw done, which caused this problem to start, and I had to get the doctor to call in a prescription to a lab to come to my apartment to draw blood so I would not miss a month.

Through the rest of 2004 I began to decline, and in February of 2005 I began feeling sick and wound up in the hospital for another surgery. I had an aneurysm in my stomach, and if not for the emergency room nurse no one would have noticed that my amylase count was up and my liver was not functioning correctly.

I began forgetting simple terms for things, and realized that I could not even add or subtract numbers in order to balance my checkbook. I had been a full-charge bookkeeper for a photo engraving company, and I had done the books for my family's dry cleaning business.

Then one morning I decided to go down to buy bread in the bakery down the block. I did not remember going there and forgot my way home. I did something really stupid. I asked a total stranger to drive me home and she did. I had a home health aide, who called my daughter and told her I was AWOL when she arrived. When my daughter came home, she made sure that I knew not to do that again, and how dangerous it was to ask a total stranger to drive me anywhere.

It was at that minute that I knew that I would no longer be able to be alone for long periods of time, and that I had to resign myself to the fact that I would lose more of my independence. My other daughter Marcia did my bills and balanced my checkbook. I forgot how to understand numbers, and even my ability to read declined.

May of 2005: I was out with my family for Mother's Day and I began feeling weak and lightheaded. I felt a pain in my back again and asked to go home. My daughter started to drive me home when my other one said, "Straight to the hospital. Obviously, her INR is off due to a new medication she is taking that did not interact well with her Coumadin."

I spent over a week in the hospital. The staff was not that great to me, and one night they left me sitting in a chair in my room and did not put me back into my bed. I could hardly walk and did not really understand what was happening. I could not reach the phone to answer it, and I did not remember how to dial it.

My daughter became concerned when I did not answer the phone, and she called the nurse's desk and made sure that I was okay. Although they did put me back in my bed after leaving me in the chair for over five hours, they did not seem to care about me at all. They even tried to convince my daughters to put me in a nursing home, and they told them they would take over my care if they did not listen. Knowing my daughter Fran, I knew that it would never happen.

She was the one they surrounded the next morning and tried to intimidate. She took out her phone and called her attorney, and explained to them that would never happen as long as she had power of attorney and was in charge of my care.

I knew that ORT was waiting for my ads for their journal. It was my job to get the ads and put the entire journal together for them. But, since getting sick and not driving anymore, how was I going to get this done? Well, there was only one way, and I knew that my daughter would not be too thrilled to get stuck running around collecting ads and money from total strangers, but we could only hope for the best. The journal had to go to the printer before the end of the next week, and since being ill I had not even put the rough draft together.

I needed to get the president's message and the messages from the other officers in the organization. I needed to get the ads from the storeowners and any city or state officials that wanted an ad in the journal. I also needed the In Memory information or any other announcements that members wanted to place in the journal.

Still remembering certain things, but not everything, I told my daughter the best way that I could what needed to be done. Instead of getting upset, she took an older journal and used it as the basis for the new one. She took my notes and wrote down all of the people who had paid for the ads or memory pages, and wrote down those that were already sent in and those she needed to get.

Never doing this before, she knew that she would need help, and she asked my sister Tova to help her. They both went around White Plains Road in the Bronx and got as many ads as they could from the storeowners where they both shopped. Then, Tova called all of her contacts in the Democratic Club and those she'd met when we both did voter's registration and worked at the polls on election day, and they both managed to get the journal together. This would be the last one that I was able to do.

This was the real start of the decline due to the disease. It was beginning to slowly eat away at my senses and my brain. I could barely use the phone, and I became totally incontinent after a week at the hospital. My daughter had to buy supplies in order to keep me clean and dry at home. When she was finally able to get me Medicaid services, no one told her that many of the supplies were not covered. She laid out, along with my other daughter, thousands of dollars for supplies and for my home care. Although she was able to get me twelve hours of Medicaid home health services, both of my daughters had to pay thousands a month for the other ninety-six hours a week. This was upsetting to them and to me. Even though I was starting to understand less and less, I knew that both of them were stressed out and looked worried all the time.

As time went on, I did not understand how costly the expenses were going to be. I heard numbers like $1,500 a week, and sometimes more. I saw my daughters looking upset and so despondent that I wished I could take away the sadness in their eyes and bring back the smiles. When in 2006 my daughter Frani finally got VNS to agree to the split shift home health aides, I did not know what that meant, but I could see the strain and the sadness finally melt away.

Unfortunately, the fight was not over yet. VNS tried to take away my aides in January of 2007, but fortunately my daughter Fran got right on it and made sure that did not happen. I did not understand how, but she did it with help of some very important people and a great lawyer.

Throughout the past two years, my daughters have been working hard to keep my home care in place and make sure that there are no changes. It has been a struggle for them both, and it only promises to get harder. I have many medical issues that need to be addressed on a daily basis, and I have many dietary issues that have to be met. The aides have to read labels to make sure that certain things are not in any of the foods I eat, and they have to make sure that I am not black and blue or bruised, as well as watching for any swelling on my body.

At the present time I can barely speak in sentences, and my speech is often incoherent. But, I am here and I hope that someday soon there will be a cure, so that just maybe there will be one more miracle, and everyone who has the disease will be cured and able to live their lives as independent people once more.

Ruth—*In her own words*

How do you say goodbye when you have so many more hello's inside of you longing to come out? What do you do when everyone around you is talking, and you have no idea what they are saying? How do you react when your family, children, and friends are around you, and you have to keep your own private scorecard in your mind as to who they are, but never quite figure it out? What do you do when the world around you seems to be fading because something has overtaken your mind, and there is no way to stop it?

Quicksand will send you down a deep hole real fast and you won't know what hit you, and there is no way to pull yourself out unless you get help real fast. A tsunami runs its own course and the devastation and the havoc created is insurmountable. An earthquake strikes and you are left homeless, helpless, and injured. But, when your mind is taken over by a hidden force that slowly seeps within the crevices of your brain and takes hold of your every thought, leaving you helpless to fight even though you try, life takes on a different meaning and you begin to forget why you are still here.

Think about this as I write in my journal while I still can, or I dictate my thoughts, making sure they are conveyed the right way for everyone to understand what happens when this dreaded disease invades your brain with no invitation, no "Cordially attend the destruction of my brain free of charge," no warning, just slowly and methodically taking over my brain and leaving nothing.

Take a magic slate and create a design, message, picture, or just write a letter on it, and then take the slate and flip it up. What's left? NOTHING! Whatever you created is gone and will never return unless you reproduce it once more. Your mind, after a while when this disease is finally done destroying it, will be no more than what is left after you lift that magic slate's cover and obliterate your work. Like a raging inferno that starts with a small spark or is ignited with a match, your mind disintegrates and nothing is left. Alzheimer's is the name of this uninvited guest, who takes hold of your every thought and could care less about the end result. My name is RUTHIE: It's too late!

Fran

My mom is at home and she has four home health aides who are amazing. Her doctors have done all they can do for her. There are no new treatments out there, and no new medications approved by the FDA to help her or anyone else with this disease. I know that there are medications being tested in foreign countries and many types of research being done, and not here in New York City but in other states. I only hope that someday our government decides to really put some money and effort into curing or at least halting this disease by giving more money for Alzheimer's research. I just came from my mom's house, and I wanted to tell her about my two books, and my second being showcased or spotlighted on "Author's Events" by Ernie Johnson. I did tell her, and she smiled. I know that somewhere inside of her she is proud of me.

Ruth

The day is clear, but I realize that somehow my world is going dimmer and dimmer. My daughter hoped and prayed that the aides would never want to leave my side, and although I recognized their faces, I did not know their names. One is tall and thin and pretty. One is heavy and eats a lot. One is kind and sweet, and the others are funny and take great care of me. There are six, and my daughter calls them by name, but all I know is that when the tall and pretty one comes my daughter Marcia came that day, too.

Now she is missing in my life, and I don't know why she stopped coming. Somehow I knew that my daughter was missing or something happened. Her picture was right above my chair, and I could not understand why she never came. People were coming to my apartment and had tears in their eyes, hugged me and Fran, but I just thought they were happy to see us. Then I heard whispers and they asked what happened to Marcia, and even though my mind was not that sharp, I realized that she had died. I said out loud to no one in particular, "SHE'S GONE. NOT COMING BACK!" Everyone just stared and could not believe what I'd said, and at that moment I knew that I was going to join her very soon. Things started to take a bad turn, and I was spending too many hours in the emergency room, and I knew it was taking a toll on Fran and Jeff. I knew that my son had his own issues, but would manage to come and see me with my grandsons, and he did. With him living a great distance away, the burden of care was and always has been mostly on Fran. And you could see at times the stress in her face, but her everlasting words always came through: No matter what, mom, you will return home.

Fran

Remember: not everyone can make and keep the promise that I did. Not all facilities are poor; there are some that are great, but it's up to you to do your homework, have a family meeting to gain support, and ask who will be able to care for your parent or loved one when you are not there or at work. You need to visit the care facility and ask questions and see the patients in many different settings. Ask other people who are visiting what they think about the facility, and then go online and check out complaints and reviews before deciding. Home care can be expensive when you have to pay for some services, and even when paying someone you have to make sure you do background checks or the agency does. The first few times you need to be there to supervise and explain what the needs are of the patient. I did, and at times I would pop in when least expected to make sure that my mom was in good hands. When necessary, I did change agencies and aides, before I was blessed with Joyce, Joan, Tessa, Patricia, Getty, Laurel, and Loretta. To those of you who are caregivers and those home health aides, remember you are saving a life, keeping someone alive, and all you do is special, and you COUNT!

Three weeks before the end, my mom was taken back to the hospital where she would spend her remaining days. In the ER the staff did their best to try and revive her several times. At times she appeared to be alert while other times staring off into space, and yet throughout her journey and life, she never forgot who she was. With the gravity of her condition, the hospital placed her in ICU. One of the interns resented the move and said something that I will never forget: "Why waste a space for someone that might not make it even one day? Why not give the space to someone else with a less serious illness that might benefit from the care in ICU?" I saw red! I was fuming, and found the head nurse and resident on the floor, and things moved faster as she was taken to ICU and the intern taken into a private room. Needless to say, his attitude changed but his words rang out, and I had difficulty with him even caring or going near my mom. I expressed my concerns and another intern replaced him.

The ICU was small. They limited the times you could visit, but the care and the doctors in charge were exemplary, and often allowed me to remain there even after visiting hours, knowing the gravity of my mom's situation and condition. When after one week they realized that they did whatever was feasible, she was moved to the ninth floor for the final two weeks of her life, where the care was just as outstanding, and the nurses, doctors, and physician assistants explained their hopes for my mom. But at this point, she had a breathing tube, and their goal was to try and get her to breathe on her own, so they opted for a tracheotomy. Being Ruthie, it bothered her that she could not really talk, and the feeding tube annoyed her but, with her usual flare, she made her voice heard through mannerisms and trying to speak even with the tracheotomy. Her spunk and spirit never died, until March 6 at 10 P.M., when the hospital called us to come because they did not think she would survive much longer.

The night was the longest in my life. The fear in my eyes, my heart, and even in the physician assistant's eyes, who seemed lost and did not know how to proceed at times, let me know that I was now spending time with my mom in her final hours. My husband and I remained there all night and into the morning, when at 9:30 A. M. on March 7, 2011, she took her final breath, looked at me, and said "NO MORE!" She closed her eyes for the last time. Watching her go was hard. Knowing she was at peace gave me comfort, and then telling my brother and my family…as you can imagine, some thought it was for the best, while others said they would miss her forever. Some family members had always been there for her and for me, while others said they could not deal with seeing her as a different person than she was when they were growing up. But throughout it all, she was still and would always be RUTHIE!

To my cousin Susan, who was always there and still is for me, you are the second sister I always wanted. To my sister, Marcia, you were my support and rock throughout it all. I miss you everyday. To my brother, Keith, for his constant calls and even coming from a long distance to see my mom, I hope that we can continue to be close. To my husband, Jeff, I could not have kept my promise and stood my ground without you.

Chapter Nine

What I Learned on This Journey

Fran

For those who are caregivers, I hope that the next part of this book will help guide you through the journey you have chosen to take.

Caregivers are special people: Tips to help you survive

As the primary and only caregiver for my mom, who had Alzheimer's, I have had to develop different ways to keep myself active and my mind stimulated. All too often as a caregiver we become so immersed in taking care of the needs of the person who is ill that we forget about ourselves. When you make the decision to care for the family member at home, you are really taking on a challenge of Herculean proportion. Every day is different, and every challenge unique, and must be handled differently but with kindness and care.

When a person has Alzheimer's, the hardest thing to deal with is their forever changing erratic behaviors. He/she can be calm one minute, and out of control or violent the next. These behaviors tend to put a lot of stress and strain on the caregiver. Here are some ways that I found worked with my mom, and might help others deal with these behaviors.

Discussions and Talking: Tips

I'm going to use the pronouns "her" and "she" in my tips but, of course, my recommendations pertain to anyone with Alzheimer's disease or dementia.

A. I find that speaking slowly and softly in a calm voice does help to calm the person down.
B. Speaking in simple sentences and short phrases does help.
C. Repeating something in different ways sometimes helps her to understand what she needs to do. It is as simple as saying "Open" or "Open your mouth" instead of "Eat this," or trying to explain to her that she needs to eat.

D. I always call her by her first name or, of course, mom, to get her attention. At this point, she still knows who she is when you call her. She does not always say her name or respond verbally when asked who she is.

E. Always be positive and smile at her. Do not let her think that you are angry. She is not at fault, and cannot control or help her behaviors.

Cleaning and Dressing Her

1. The one thing that is hard when trying to keep a person with this illness clean is trying to bathe her. Fortunately, I do have four home health aides that are great. But, they often ask me to assist them when she is hard to handle. They told me they have a daily schedule for bathing, feeding, and getting her dressed.

2. Always be kind and gentle when bathing her, and always pick out clothing that is easy to put on, and easy to get off.

3. Explain what you are going to do and why, even if she does not fully understand.

4. Always make sure that you have the soap, sponges, and the showerhead ready. It might be better if she sits on a bench in the tub, which makes it safer

and prevents her from falling. A railing on the side prevents her from getting out by herself.

5. If a shower is not possible, using a handheld showerhead, or a sponge bath might be the next best option.

6. Dressing the person is often more difficult. You need to get her dressed at the same time each day. The one thing that I know is important is whether or not she is going out, she should get dressed every day. She needs to have her hair and nails groomed and cleaned, and look as normal as possible.

7. If she is still able to choose what to wear, then let her have the choice. It will make her feel better and show that she is being treated with respect and dignity.

8. I find that elastic waists in pants are easier for the aides to dress her.

9. Slip-on shoes are much easier than tying knots in sneakers or walking shoes.

Eating: this can be a real challenge, especially in the late stages of the illness. Here are some tips for making that easier for you as the caregiver.

1. If she is having trouble chewing certain foods or if the foods are hard to swallow, you can puree the foods in a blender, turning it into a softer

consistency to be eaten. I find that when the aides make chicken soup and add pasta, potatoes, and other vegetables, it is easier for my mom to eat the soup if it is pureed in a blender.

2. If the person is aware of what she might want to eat, you might give her some choices. I would limit the choices to two, so as not to overwhelm her with too much decision-making.

3. You need to choose foods that allow her to eat independently and, hopefully, without having to be fed or needing too much assistance.

4. The one thing that is vital is that since the amount of foods or food she consumes will eventually decrease as the disease progresses, you need to make sure that she drinks a lot of fluids to prevent dehydration.

5. It is necessary to make sure that there is nothing in the foods that is difficult to swallow, because as the disease progresses it will become harder for her to swallow, and you need to help her avoid choking.

Incontinence: You need to make sure that the nurse or caregiver assigned to your loved-one's case knows which home care agency will provide the supplies needed on a monthly basis, rather than having you pay for them out of pocket. You should follow these tips, too.

1. Set up a daily schedule for her to go to the bathroom. The aides change my mom every two hours to prevent rashes, sores, and chafing. They make sure that they have A&D ointment on hand, as well as Desitin or Balmex, in order to make sure that she does not get any sores of any kind.

2. If she starts to fidget and gets restless, it is often a sign that she should be taken to the bathroom on the spot. (If still capable of using the bathroom.)

3. Be aware that accidents will happen, and you need to stay calm and be understanding. The first time this happened to my mom, she was in the hospital, and did realize that she was forgetting to go to the bathroom. She often rang for the nurse, who never came. I think part of her problem came because she just didn't get there in time, in addition to the poor staffing of people who did not really concern themselves with patients that were incontinent. I know that they do get busy and backed up, but it became apparent that this was going to be an issue. She did not want to wear the diapers and preferred to use the bedpan or the commode.

4. To prevent nighttime accidents, limit the amount of fluids she drinks before going to bed.

5. If she is aware that she needs to use the bathroom, and you are going on a long trip, you might want

to learn where the rest stops are located on your route so you can stop. It's a good idea to take extra clothes in case of an accident. I know that with my mom, we made sure that she had an adult diaper on top of her underwear to prevent this issue from causing her any embarrassment.

Sleeping and Wandering

1. My mom does not sleep throughout the night. When we first found out she had the illness, she even tried to leave the apartment and go shopping in the middle of the night. She left one morning and walked to the bakery to get bread. Not really knowing where she was and why she did that, she stopped a stranger in a car to drive her home. Lucky for her, the person knew her. When I got the call from the aide who was late in coming to care for her that she was missing and finally found, I realized that we needed more help, and more hours of it, too.

2. Make sure that you enroll her in the Safe Return Program from the Alzheimer's Association. This is a program that helps you register her with the necessary information needed to contact you in case she gets lost. You receive two bracelets and a necklace, plus labels. You can sew the labels into her clothing, and you can wear one bracelet and

she wears the other so, in case of emergency, both parties can be helped and contacted.

3. Keep a photo of her in your wallet and on a table in your living room and in her home, in case the she becomes lost and an ID needs to be made by the police.

4. Keep a list of her medications and other vital information, including how much medication and how often the pills are taken. Post this information on the refrigerator, along with a plan of care if you have home care.

5. Make sure that you put sharp objects out of her reach. Unplug toaster ovens and microwaves, because she might forget to turn them off when she tries to use them. Prepare meals for her and leave them in the refrigerator to be warmed by you, or an aide. Make sure that the locks on the front door are too high for her to open. Make sure if there is a back door that it is secured and locked, and cannot be opened. You might want to have a keyed deadbolt or an additional lock that is too high for her to reach placed on the front door of a house or an apartment. You might even add a chain.

6. Alzheimer's patients get disoriented and cannot tell the difference between day and night. Assure

her that she is in a safe place and safe environment. Never yell, scold, or make her feel like she did something wrong. Remember: It is the disease, NOT the person, causing these behaviors.

7. As the disease gets worse, she might begin seeing things, hearing things, and having delusions. Hallucinations are when the person sees, hears, smells, and feels that something or someone is there, but it really is not.

8. Delusions are beliefs that are false, in which the person is so totally convinced that something is happening she cannot be dissuaded.

9. Never yell at her, and always assure her that you are taking care of getting rid of whatever is upsetting her. I remember my Aunt Tova was given Haldol in the hospital and thought she saw squirrels on the ceiling of her room, and that she left old bread and cheese in her freezer. She made my cousin call me, and I told her that I would get rid of the bread and cheese, and I was right there to take care of the squirrels. She even told me she saw my Uncle Irving and my father, Doc, who had been gone a long time.

Chapter Ten

Many Hands: Understanding Goes A Long Way!

You count, too!

Remember to make time for yourself and your family. Do not neglect your personal appearance or your personal needs. Make sure that you take time for yourself every day. Make sure that you develop an interest or a hobby, and set aside time, as I do, to pursue what makes you happy.

Make sure that when you feel stressed, you take a break and go out for a walk, rest, or just read a book. You cannot be on call twenty-four hours a day. Make sure that if your loved one needs an aide, you get the services needed in order to help yourself maintain some semblance of a normal life, and time with your family.

I know that there is always one person in a family who gets the burden of the care. That, of course, is not right and not fair. However, you need to make sure that you get to go away even overnight or on a weekend in order to rejuvenate yourself and feel better. You deserve it! I know I need time off from giving my mom her meds every morning and every night. I sometimes feel like I am wearing a straitjacket that needs to be loosened. I wish that I could go away for a week, but I know that is not in the cards. No one wants the responsibility of dealing with the agencies, the meds, and the aides. It gets tough!

But, as I have been told so many times, "You are doing the right thing, and someday you will be blessed and rewarded." I know that I can look myself in the mirror and know that I have nothing to feel guilty about, and I know that I am trying my best to keep my mom at home. I know that a person with Alzheimer's disease has a limited lifestyle. I promised my mom that I would never put her in a facility of any kind, and I will not break that promise.

How do you know that you need to get help for a loved one?

When my mom went shopping by herself to the bakery one morning and asked a total stranger to drive her home, I knew things were taking a downward slide. Asking her why she would accept a ride with someone she did not know, she looked at me and said, "I have no idea what you are talking about. That lady is my friend." She was a friend whose name she did not know, nor did I.

When my mom began to exhibit the following behaviors, my brother, sister, and I realized we needed to get her more help than the three of us could provide. The following list of behaviors indicate the need for doing research and a lot of legwork to make sure that you get the right help for your parent or loved one.

1. When someone is unable to remember things.
2. Asking or repeating the same question or story multiple times.
3. Getting lost in familiar places.
4. Being unable to follow and understand directions.
5. Getting disoriented about time, people, and places.
6. Neglecting personal safety, hygiene, and nutrition.
7. As in my mom's case, asking a stranger for a ride home.
8. Wandering the neighborhood, and not remembering his/her own address.
9. Forgetting names and places.

10. As in my mom's case, taking meds more than the required number of times a day.

Kindness tips:

1. Always say good morning when entering a patient's room.
2. Address the patient by name, and tell the patient your name.
3. SMILE!
4. Explain the task you are going to perform before you do it, and explain the task as you are performing. Patients are often leery or afraid of strangers, and need to feel confident and safe with you.
5. If a patient needs assistance bathing, eating, or walking, help him/her, and do not leave before the task is completed.
6. Patients that need help eating: You need to make sure that the person eats and is fed. Make sure that you do not leave the tray untouched, and if you have to feed the patient, you need to do it with kindness and patience.
7. Ask the patient if he/she needs help dressing or assistance going to breakfast, or any other area of the home or hospital.
8. If you are bringing magazines or books, allow the person to choose.

9. Never speak to a patient as if he/she is a small child.
10. Speak to people with respect and as an adult.
11. Make sure that the person's environment is safe.
12. Make sure you have a list of things that need to be done for that person, and complete them.
13. Meet with other volunteers and discuss their successes.
14. When you speak to a patient, make sure that you make eye contact and have his/her attention.
15. Speak at eye level, and speak clearly.
16. Use simple and direct statements.
17. Never raise your voice.
18. Include the person in your conversation. Talk to the person, not at the person.
19. Never speak to the person as if he/she is a third party in the same room.
20. Listen to the concerns of the patient, and show a lot of understanding.
21. Never leave a patient in distress.

Your role as a volunteer is important and valuable.

There are many jobs that are special and important. Never think that because you are not getting paid to be a volunteer it hinders your value, importance, or role.

Many of the people you come in contact with have no family members visiting, are afraid to be alone, and might look forward to your visit, no matter how long or short, as the highlight of their day.

Just walking into the patient's room and knowing that you are there to speak to him/her or perform a needed task can be the difference between someone giving up on life and feeling needed and special.

Everything you do has value and a purpose. Never allow anyone to tell you that you do not have to work or volunteer on a specific day, because it does not matter since you are not getting paid. Work ethics need to be adhered to. Volunteer positions can lead to paying ones—you never know. Your time is valuable, and what you are doing to help someone in these facilities is worth more than all the money in the world. Never sell short what you are doing.

Most important and final notes:

- Remember to be sensitive to the needs of the person.
- Understand that the diagnosis is upsetting, and show compassion.
- Communicate with the Alzheimer's patient.
- Have an upbeat and positive attitude.

- Understand and learn how to handle behavior changes.
- Expect that the patient will have memory loss, and over time even more.
- Get support for yourself, and make sure that you do not neglect yourself.
- Speak in short, familiar words, phrases, and simple sentences. Repeat yourself if necessary. Stay calm.
- Allow the person plenty of time to answer. If the person does not respond or answer, reword the question.
- Ask only one question at a time.
- Never give negative instructions. Do not say "Don't" or "Never" or "You'd better not." Say "Let's try this" or "Let's go over here."
- We are in this together!
- Work together and help the patient understand.
- Mobility is important, and your assistance makes a big difference.
- Shopping can help him/her stay focused and feel useful.
- Your visit and care makes all the difference.
- Helping someone with a smile makes a difference in the other person's life.
- Remember: Everything you do matters and is special. **Caregivers are special, and unique!**

Resources that I used for this book:

www.alz.org

https://alzfdn.org

www.nia.nih.gov

www.nia.nih.gov/Alzheimers

www.nia.nih.gov/Alzheimers/Publications/
caregiverguide.htm#intro

www.nia.nih.gov/Healthinformation/Publications/
forgetfulness.htm

http://www.mayoclinic.org

https://jwa.org/thisweek/oct/12/1927/womens-
american-ort

About the Author

Fran Lewis is author of 13 books (see www.amazon.com/Fran-Lewis/e/B002F8Z87U), including three children's books: *My Name is Bertha, Bertha Speaks Out,* and *Bertha Fights Back;* and four books in her *Faces Behind the Stones* series. She wrote two prior books related to Alzheimer's disease, titled *Memories are Precious: Alzheimer's Journey—Ruth's Story;* and *Sharp As A Tack or Scrambled Eggs: Which Describes Your Brain?*

Fran has three masters degrees, and a Ph.D. in supervision and administration. She worked in the New York City public schools as the reading and writing staff developer for more than 36 years, during which she also served as musical director for shows and ran the school's newspaper. She is a member of Who's Who of America's Teachers and Who's Who of America's Executives from Cambridge.

Fran writes reviews for authors upon request and for several websites. She hosts a radio show on http://www.blogtalkradio.com/fran-lewis, in which she interviews *New York Times,* and Indie Book Award winning authors.

Fran Lewis

Photo Album

Ruth as a young girl

Ruth and her husband, "Doc"

Ruth and her family

Ruth's brother Kenny with his wife, Tommy

Ruth with her sister Tova and friends

Ruth with her friend Florence and sister Tova

Tova and Ruth at PS 67 in the Bronx

PTA PS 67, of which Ruth was president

Ruth's daughter Marcia

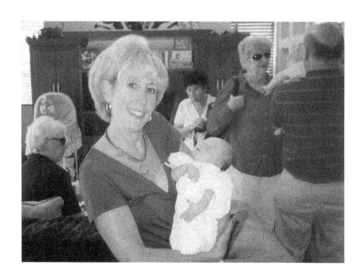

Friends from National Council of Jewish Women

Ruth

Ruth with daughter Marcia, and
daughter-in-law, Marcia

Ruth's family getting ready for Chanukah

Fran and her husband, Jeff

Ruth's son Keith, daughter-in-law Marcia,
and grandson DJ

129

Ruth's son Keith with his wife, Marcia, and
their boys, Josh and DJ

Fran and Marcia with Ruth at City Island

Marcia and her son Jason

Marcia's daughter Jamie and son Jason

Marcia's son Jason with his wife, Tammy

Marcia's daughter Jamie with her husband, Rob

Jason and Tammy's oldest daughter Casey,
and Jamie and Rob's oldest daughter Dani
(they're both 21 now)

CPSIA information can be obtained
at www.ICGtesting.com
Printed in the USA
BVHW041919200120
569951BV00011B/94